Simply DOS, 2nd Edition

Kris Jamsa

Osborne **McGraw-Hill**
2600 Tenth Street
Berkeley, California 94710
U.S.A.

For information on software, translations, or book distributors outside of the U.S.A.,
please write to Osborne **McGraw-Hill** at the above address.

Simply DOS, 2nd Edition

234567890 DOC 99876543

ISBN 0-07-881914-8

Acknowledgments

It won't take you long to realize that *Simply DOS*, Second Edition is a very special book. Filled with hundreds of illustrations resulting in unique page layouts, *Simply DOS* required the expertise and cooperation of a team of professionals.

After I submitted the initial manuscript, seemingly tireless copy and technical editors began their efforts on the text, using countless red markers to ensure the book's correctness and ease of use. Next, a staff of typesetters entered the modifications under the watchful eyes of proofreaders. Throughout this time, Susie C. Kim transformed my rough sketches into the beautiful illustrations that fill the pages of this book. Finally, a team of designers had the difficult task of merging the text and illustrations into the form you see today.

The list of contributors to this book is too long to permit me to express my gratitude to each. I hope the Osborne team feels my appreciation for their unselfish contributions to this book.

Kris Jamsa

Acquisitions Editor *Allen L. Wyatt, Sr.*

Associate Editor **Project Editor**
Emily Rader *Nancy McLaughlin*

Copy Editor
Kathryn Hashimoto

Indexer
Phil Schmauder

Proofreader
Audrey Johnson

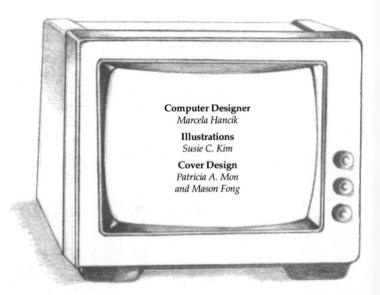

Computer Designer
Marcela Hancik

Illustrations
Susie C. Kim

Cover Design
*Patricia A. Mon
and Mason Fong*

Contents

Special Offer

One of the greatest frustrations users experience when working with DOS is forgetting a command. **DOS HELP** is a software program you can copy to your hard disk; it contains all of the answers to your DOS questions.

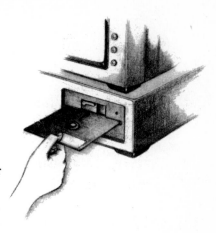

DOS HELP displays a friendly menu that summarizes all the DOS commands. By highlighting a command with your arrow keys and pressing ENTER, you can discover command specifics, view common examples of the command in use, and read tips that make you even more effective.

Every computer user should have a copy of **DOS HELP!**

Ordering Information

Domestic Orders:
Please send $24.95 (includes shipping and handling) to the address below. For fastest service, please send a money order or cashier's check. Please allow 2 to 3 weeks for delivery.

Foreign Orders:
Please send $29.95 (USD; includes shipping and handling) to the address below. For fastest service, please send an international money order. Please allow 4 to 6 weeks for delivery.

(Credit card orders not accepted)

- -

Order Today!

Please send _____ copies of **DOS HELP**. Enclosed is my check/money order for $ _____

Name: _____

Address: _____

City: _____ State: _____ ZIP: _____

Country: _____ Phone: _____

Please send your order with payment to:

Concept Software
P.O. Box 26981
Las Vegas, NV 89126

Getting Comfortable with Your Computer's Hardware

Your computer hardware is made up of the keyboard, screen, chassis and printer, and the cables that tie them all together. Although your computer uses complex electronic components, you do not necessarily have to understand how the hardware works in order to make good use of it. In many cases, you must simply know how to turn on your equipment, which is usually as easy as turning on your television.

Like your television, your computer's hardware cannot be harmed through everyday use. If you move the hardware with care and do not place other objects on top, your computer will last a long time.

Almost every personal computer today has a monitor, a keyboard, a printer, a chassis, hard and floppy disk drives, and a mouse. This chapter introduces you to these hardware devices.

Monitor

The monitor is your computer's video screen. It allows you to view information displayed by your software programs. For example, if you are using a word processing program to type a letter, your monitor enables you to view each line of the letter as you type it.

Almost every computer monitor today has an on-off switch and two or three knobs that allow you to adjust the picture's sharpness and contrast. In addition, your monitor has a power cable and a video cable. The power cable either plugs into a wall outlet or into the back of your computer chassis. The video cable plugs into the back of the chassis and carries the signals necessary for displaying images.

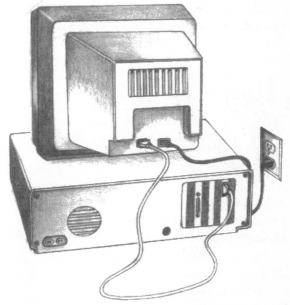

Keyboard

In order to perform useful work on your computer, you must be able to enter information and commands. The keyboard has a key layout similar to that of a typewriter, enabling you to type letters, numbers, and punctuation symbols. If you do not know how to type, relax. Typing on a computer is much easier than typing on a typewriter, because you can quickly and easily correct your mistakes.

Several different styles of keyboards are available with computers. The one shown here is the most common. Examine your keyboard and you will find additional keys not found on a typewriter. On the right side is a set of keys numbered zero through nine, as well as several mathematical keys labeled +, –, /, and *. These keys comprise the *numeric keypad*. If you are running a program that requires you to enter several numbers, you can use the numeric keypad to quickly type the numbers, just as you would use a 10-key adding machine.

The keyboard's numeric keypad is similar to a 10-key adding machine.

Your keyboard also has keys with arrows pointing up, down, left, and right, as well as keys labeled PGUP and PGDN. These keys are called *cursor movement keys* or *cursor control keys*, or simply *cursor keys*. If you use a word processor to create a memorandum or a report, you can use the cursor keys to move through the document. If you use a spreadsheet program, such as Lotus 1-2-3 or Quattro Pro, you can use the cursor keys to move from one row or column to another.

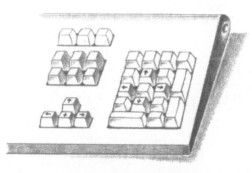

Most word processing programs let you use the cursor keys to move the cursor through your document.

If your numeric keypad is the only place where cursor keys appear, you can press the key labeled NUMLOCK to switch between the use of numbers or the use of the cursor keys. The first time you press NUMLOCK, a light on your keyboard indicates that the numbers on the numeric keypad are selected. When you press NUMLOCK a second time, the light is turned off, meaning that the cursor keys are active.

Notice the keys labeled F1, F2, F3, and so on. These are called *function keys.* The location of these keys depends on your style of keyboard.

The software programs you run will often enable

Locations of the function keys on commonly used keyboards

these keys to perform specific functions. For example, pressing F10 while using a word processing program may direct the program to print the current document. The roles and purposes of the function keys depend on the program currently in use.

Chassis

Your computer's chassis houses the disk drives and the electronics that make your computer work. The primary electronic component found in the chassis is the microprocessor, or *CPU*—short for *central processing unit*. The CPU is essentially the computer's electronic brain. Common CPU types include the 8088, 80286, 80386, and 80486. Each processor type has a different operating speed and different capabilities. Referring to a machine as a "486 machine" indicates the type of processor used (in this case, the 80486 type).

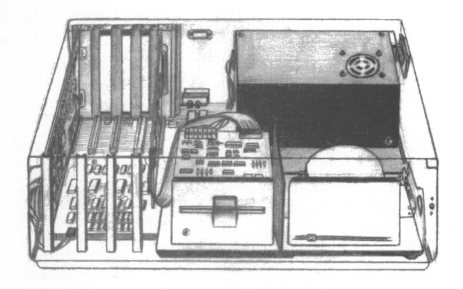

In addition to housing the CPU, the chassis contains your computer's memory or *RAM* (short for *random access memory*), as well as the interface boards that enable your computer to communicate with its monitor and printer.

To insert a new board into your computer chassis, unplug your computer, carefully remove the chassis cover, then gently insert the board into an expansion slot.

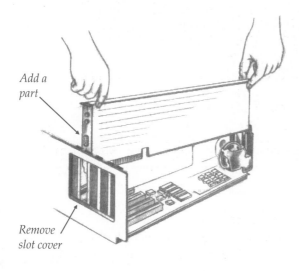

Add a part

Remove slot cover

Opening the computer chassis is seldom necessary. Generally, the only time you would ever need to do this is after purchasing a new piece of hardware (such as a modem or laser printer) that requires inserting a board into an expansion slot inside the computer. You might feel more comfortable having someone else install a new device, although it is generally a simple task to do yourself. First, always unplug the computer from the wall, then unscrew and remove the chassis lid. Finally, insert the board into the slot. Detailed instructions should be provided with each device or board that you need to install. All the devices discussed in this chapter connect to the computer at the back of the chassis. If you examine the back of the chassis,

you will find
several connecting
plugs called *ports*.
Each device connects
to a specific port.
Examining the
plug on the end of
a device's cable
usually helps you
match the plug to
the correct port.

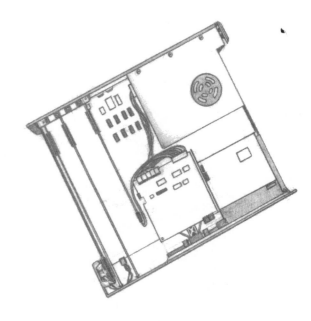

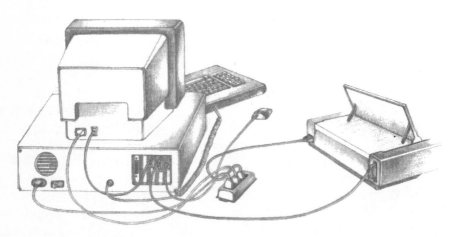

Your computer's chassis also has its own power cable and on-off switch
in addition to the ports that allow connection to other devices.

Printer

A printer outputs on paper the work you do with various programs. The result is often referred to as *hard copy*. While using a word processing program, for example, you can instruct your printer to create a hard copy of a letter, memo, or report. Just as there are several different types of computers that you can choose from, there are also many types of printers available, each with varying speeds and capabilities. The two most common are tractor-feed printers and laser printers.

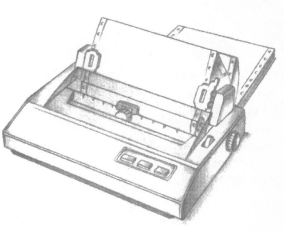

The two most common types of printers are tractor-feed and laser printers.

    Tractor-feed printers are so named because they use a tractor-like mechanism to pull each sheet of paper through the printer. *Laser printers* produce high-quality documents quickly by using technology similar to that used in a photocopy machine. The only difference is that a photocopy machine uses lights and lenses to create an image, while a laser printer receives

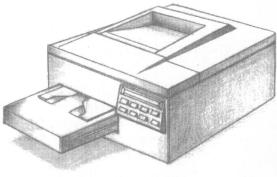

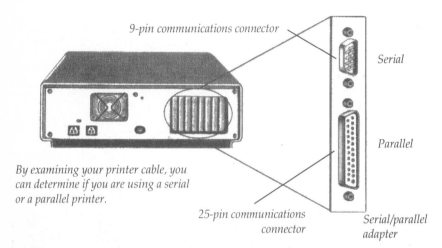

9-pin communications connector

Serial

Parallel

By examining your printer cable, you can determine if you are using a serial or a parallel printer.

25-pin communications connector

Serial/parallel adapter

images directly from a computer. All types of printers perform the same basic task—producing a hard copy of your work.

Like the monitor and the computer chassis, the printer has its own power cable and on-off switch. Depending on what type of printer you have, it will attach to either a *serial port* or a *parallel port* at the back of your computer's chassis.

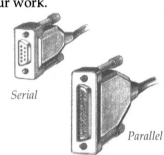

Serial

Parallel

Disks and Disk Drives

Computers use magnetically treated disks for storing information. Suppose that you are using a word processor to create a large report. You may only get the first few pages typed before you need to leave your computer or begin working on something else. By saving your document to a disk, you can easily resume your work at a later time.

The computer stores your information by magnetizing it to the disk. Saving information on a disk is much like recording music on a cassette tape. Like music on tape, the information stored on your disk remains there until you erase it or record over it.

The two types of computer disks are *hard disks* and *floppy disks*. A hard disk resides in your computer's chassis and, for purposes of this discussion, is non-removable. A floppy disk, however, is easily inserted and removed from the floppy disk drive.

Floppy Disks

Depending on your computer hardware, you may be using 3 1/2-inch or 5 1/4-inch floppy disks, or both. Because it is enclosed in a hard plastic case, a 3 1/2-inch floppy disk is better protected from accidental damage than a 5 1/4-inch disk.

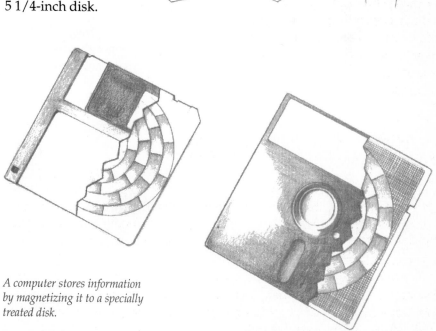

A computer stores information by magnetizing it to a specially treated disk.

The following rules will help you protect your floppy disks:

Avoid writing on a disk label once it is attached to a disk. In so doing, you may damage the disk's contents. Get into the habit of writing on the labels *before* attaching them to your floppy disks. (Should you forget to do this, use a felt-tipped pen—*not* a

ballpoint pen or pencil—to write on the fastened disk label.) If you must change a label, remove the existing label *gently*, or place the new label on top of the old one.

When you have finished using a 5 1/4-inch floppy disk, always place the disk back in its protective envelope.

Never touch a disk's magnetic surface.

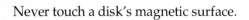

Never bend a floppy disk or try to force it into a disk drive.

Store your floppy disks in a safe location, preferably in a protective storage container.

Do not smoke near your floppy disks.

Never place your disks near magnetic or powerful electronic equipment (such as photocopy machines, typewriters, or telephones).

Do not expose your disks to excessive heat or cold.

Always make backup copies of the information on your disks, and store the backups in a safe place.

Protecting Information Stored on Floppy Disks

Recall that information you store on a disk remains there until you either erase it or write over it with new information. To protect important data that you do not wish to change, you should *write protect* the disk. Write

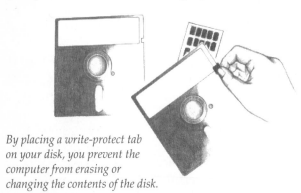

protecting prevents any new information from being recorded to the disk, and prevents the existing contents of the disk from being changed or erased. If you examine a 5 1/4-inch disk, you will find a small notch in the disk's

By placing a write-protect tab on your disk, you prevent the computer from erasing or changing the contents of the disk.

upper-right corner. This notch is called the *write-protect notch*. When the notch is uncovered, the computer can record information on the disk, or change or delete existing information. If you cover the notch with a *write-protect tab* (provided with a box of newly purchased disks), you prevent additions, changes, or deletions to the disk. Of course, you should only apply the write-protect tab after you have stored on the disk the information that you wish to protect.

A 3 1/2-inch disk contains a *write-protect hole* that you can open or close by moving a small plastic cover. When the hole is closed, the disk drive can record information to the disk. When the hole is open, the disk's contents cannot be changed.

When you write protect a disk, the disk drive can still read the information contained on the disk—it simply can't change the disk's contents. If you have a floppy disk containing information that should never be changed, safeguard the information by write protecting the disk.

To write protect a 3 1/2-inch disk, expose the write-protect hole by sliding the plastic cover.

Inserting and Removing Floppy Disks

When you insert a disk into the disk drive, the disk label should be facing up and inserted last. If the disk does not have a label, make sure that the write-protect notch is to the left side of the disk and inserted last. If you are using a 5 1/4-inch disk, close the disk drive latch after inserting the disk. To remove a 5 1/4-inch disk from the drive, unlock the latch and gently pull the disk out.

Always insert your disk with the disk label facing up and with the disk write-protect notch on the left side. The end of the disk where these items are located should enter the drive last.

A 3 1/2-inch disk drive does not have a latch. To remove a 3 1/2-inch disk, simply press the disk drive's eject button.

Notice the small disk drive activation light on the front of each disk drive. This light comes on whenever the disk drive is reading information from or storing information to a floppy disk.

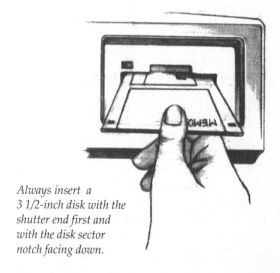

Always insert a 3 1/2-inch disk with the shutter end first and with the disk sector notch facing down.

Never open the drive latch while the drive activation light is on. Doing so may damage the disk or destroy some of its contents.

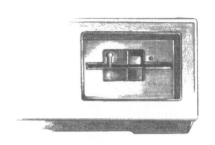

Never open your disk drive latch, or turn off your computer, while the disk drive activation light is on. (Doing so may destroy information stored on the disk.)

Hard Disks

Most computers have a hard disk that is much faster than a floppy disk, and stores far more information. When you purchase a new software package, you can copy information from the program's floppy disks to your hard disk, and then place the original floppy disks in a safe storage location. By using the hard disk, you eliminate the need to constantly shuffle floppy disks in and out of a disk drive. A hard disk actually contains several storage regions that allow you to store and organize information from a variety of sources (such as floppy disks).

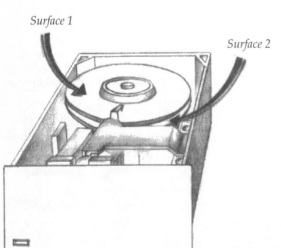

Surface 1

Surface 2

Unlike a floppy disk, which has only one recording surface, a hard disk has two or more recording surfaces.

Mouse

Many software programs (Microsoft Windows, for example) simplify your selection of menu options and other features by letting you use a *mouse* to "point" at items on the screen. If a program supports a mouse, it displays a special cursor, or *mouse pointer*. By moving the mouse around your desk, you can move the mouse pointer on the screen. When the pointer is aimed at the desired option or item, you can then select it by pressing a button on the mouse.

Unfortunately, not all programs support the mouse. However, because of the success of those programs that do, more programs are emerging that take advantage of the convenience offered by the mouse.

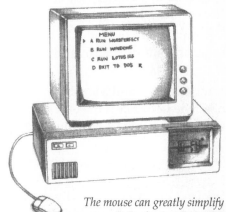

The mouse can greatly simplify your work. By moving the mouse around on your desk, you move the mouse pointer around the screen. By pressing a mouse button, you can select a specific menu option or other screen item.

Keys to Success

Hardware includes your computer's nuts, bolts, cables, and components (such as the keyboard, chassis, monitor, and printer). The keyboard is an input device that enables you to type commands and other information into the computer. The monitor is the screen that displays the information you type, as well as the computer's responses to commands you issue with the keyboard. The printer enables you to output on paper the result of your work (such as a spreadsheet or letter).

The chassis houses the computer's processor (CPU) and its disk drives. Floppy disks and hard disks allow you to store information from one work session to another. Floppy disks are removable. They come in 5 1/4- and 3 1/2-inch sizes, each requiring a matching disk drive. A hard disk, which is not removable, stores many times more information, and operates much faster, than a floppy disk.

What Do They Mean by...?

286, 386, and 486   Every PC has an electronic brain called the central processor, or CPU. Each CPU type has a unique name based on its capabilities. The original IBM PC released in 1981 had an 8088 CPU. Three years later IBM released the PC AT, which used a faster and more powerful CPU called the 80286 (or 286 for short). Developers improved the speed and capabilities of that CPU to create the 80386 (or 386). Today, an even faster and more expensive 80486 CPU is available.

Byte, Kilobyte, and Megabyte   Computers and disks store information. The term *byte* is the unit of measurement for the amount of information stored. A byte is the same as a character of information. For example, to store the word "byte" would require four characters, or bytes. The term *kilobyte* stands for "thousand bytes," and is often abbreviated as KByte, KB, or simply K. A 360K floppy disk can store 360,000 bytes. Because of their tremendous storage capacity, hard disks are described in terms of *megabytes*. One megabyte (or MB) is equivalent to 1 million bytes. A 20MB hard disk can store 20 million characters (approximately 500 single-spaced typed pages).

Memory or RAM   When your computer runs a program, it must read the program from a hard disk or a floppy disk into its electronic memory. When one program has finished running, another program can be loaded into memory, thereby replacing the first program in the computer's memory. Both programs remain unchanged on disk. The electronic memory, often referred to as RAM, exists so your computer can run programs. When you turn off your computer's power, the information stored in the electronic memory is lost. In contrast, a disk stores information even when the power is turned off. Your computer uses RAM (electronic memory) to run programs; it uses disks for long-term storage.

Getting Familiar with Computer Software

In Chapter 1 you learned that hardware includes the computer's physical components (such as the monitor, chassis, keyboard, and printer). However, hardware is only half the picture. To perform useful work, your computer must run software, or computer programs. A *software* program is simply a list of instructions that tell your computer how to accomplish a specific task. The seemingly endless list of computer programs includes word processors, database programs (which help you store and later retrieve information), spreadsheets (for numeric information), and even computer games.

Every software program is written in a programming language such as BASIC, Pascal, or C. Depending on the program's complexity, a single program might take a group of programmers several years to write! Luckily, you don't have to be a programmer, or even understand programming, to use your computer.

Software Comes Stored on Disk

When you purchase a computer program, you normally receive it on one or more floppy disks. Because software comes on disk, users often mistakenly think of floppy disks and software as the same thing. A floppy disk only stores software, just as a cassette tape stores music.

How Does Software Work?

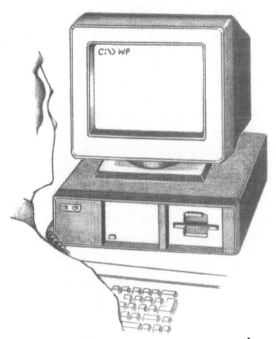

As mentioned earlier, a software program is simply a list of instructions performed by a computer. To run a specific program, simply type its name. For example, to run WordPerfect (one of the most popular word processors), simply type WordPerfect's abbreviated name, **WP**, and press ENTER. When you enter a program's name, your computer searches your disk for the program. Once your computer finds the program, it begins performing the list of instructions the program contains.

Software

Software is computer programs. Software is stored on floppy disks. Each software program has a name that is explained in the program's user's manual. To run a computer program, you simply type the program's name and press ENTER.

Where Does DOS Fit In?

Without a list of instructions, your computer won't do anything. In fact, by itself, your computer wouldn't even understand a program name you typed to run a specific program. To make your computer useful, a special program called the *disk operating system* (or *DOS*) is necessary. DOS is loaded every time your computer is turned on, allowing you to enter commands and run other programs. In general, DOS is your host while you use the computer. It is responsible for storing information on your disks and letting you print information with your printer.

Although DOS is a very powerful program with many different commands, you need to know only a few basics before putting your computer to good use. Chapter 3 discusses how to start your computer and how to recognize DOS. In Chapter 4, you will use your first DOS commands.

For now, however, understand that your computer uses hardware and software to accomplish different tasks. Software is computer programs that provide detailed instructions to the computer. When you purchase software, it comes on disk. Lastly, before you can run your software programs, your computer must run DOS, a special program that serves as your host while using your computer.

Keys to Success

Hardware is your computer's physical components, such as the keyboard, screen, and printer. Software is the term for computer programs containing the instructions that tell your hardware what to do. Working together, your computer's hardware and software let you accomplish specific tasks.

Computer programs are stored on disk. Each program has a unique name. To run a program, you simply type in the program's name and press ENTER.

DOS is a special program that runs each time your computer starts. DOS lets you run programs and store information on disk. In general, DOS is your host while you use your computer.

What Do They Mean by...?

Application and System Software   Software is categorized into one of two groups. *Application software* includes programs written to accomplish a specific task (or application), such as a word processor, spreadsheet, or database program. *System software* includes programs that are necessary for your computer to run (such as DOS) or programs that let you use a local area network. Most software falls into the application software group.

Operating System   An operating system is the first program your computer runs each time you turn on the computer. The operating system program enables your computer to use all of its hardware devices, run programs, and store files. DOS (Disk Operating System) is the most common operating system for personal computers.

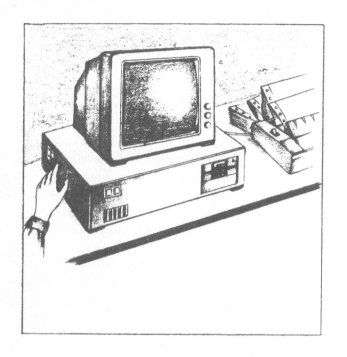

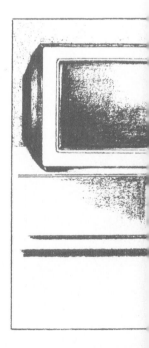

Starting Your Computer

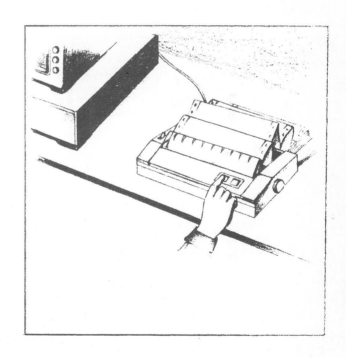

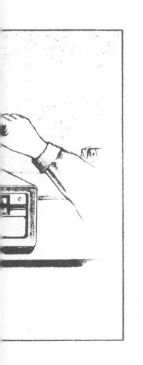

Before your computer can run programs, you must turn on your hardware (your computer, monitor, and printer), which then enables your computer to run DOS. As discussed in Chapter 2, DOS is the first program your computer must run. DOS, in turn, allows your computer to run other programs, such as your word processor or spreadsheet. Your computer manufacturer probably will have installed DOS on your computer's hard disk for you.

Before starting DOS from your hard disk, you must remove any disks from the disk drives and return them to their envelopes.

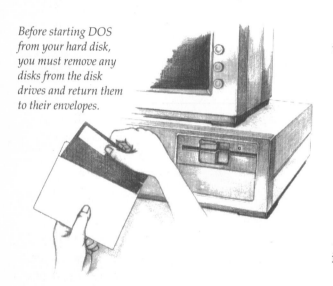

As such, remove any floppy disks that may have been left in your disk drives, and return the disks to their protective envelopes. If your computer does not have a hard disk, you need the floppy disk labeled *DOS System Disk.* Insert this disk into drive A and close the disk drive latch.

Turning On Your Computer's Power

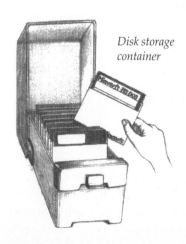

Disk storage container

As you learned in Chapter 1, you must plug in your computer, monitor, and printer individually. In addition, each of these devices has its own on-off switch. To begin, turn on each device. The order in which you turn on the devices does not matter.

When you turn on your computer, you should hear a fan start to whir. Next, your computer automatically checks several of its internal components to ensure they are in working order. As your computer performs this "self test," it may display the amount of its electronic memory (RAM) and other testing information on your monitor.

After the computer successfully finishes its self test, it automatically looks for DOS. Regardless of whether your system uses a hard disk or a floppy disk,

During its self test, your computer may display the amount of RAM available.

the computer always looks in the floppy disk drive first for a copy of DOS. You should now see one of the drive activation lights turn on. If the drive contains a disk, the computer tries to load DOS from the disk. If the drive is empty, your computer tries to load DOS from your hard disk.

Starting DOS

Later chapters will discuss how DOS can automatically run a specific program every time the computer is turned on. Experienced users often help new DOS users by customizing what the computer does when it is started up, thereby simplifying the steps you must perform when starting DOS. Depending on how DOS was installed on your computer, the steps you must follow may differ. The following discussion focuses on the most common start-up steps.

To begin, your computer may display what it thinks is the current date and wait for you to enter the actual current date:

```
Current date is Mon 04-05-1993
Enter new date (mm-dd-yy):
```

The date shown by the computer is called the *default*. If it is correct, press ENTER. This date is now used by the computer. If the default date is incorrect, type a new date using numbers for the month, day, and year in the form *mm-dd-yy*. For example, to enter the date December 31, 1993, enter **12-31-93**:

```
Current date is Mon 04-05-1993
Enter new date (mm-dd-yy): 12-31-93 <ENTER>
```

If you mistype a letter, use BACKSPACE to erase the letter, then type the correct letter. If you type the date incorrectly and press ENTER, DOS will display an error message and prompt you again to enter the correct date.

Next, your computer may display what it thinks is the current time, and prompt you to enter a new time.

```
Current time is 12:23:39.82p
Enter new time:
```

The computer uses a 24-hour (or military) clock. Table 3-1 lists the 24-hour times. If the default system time (displayed by the computer) is correct, simply press ENTER. If the time is incorrect, type the new time in the form *hh:mm*, where *hh* is the current hour (using the 24-hour format) and *mm* represents the current minutes. For example, to set the clock to 7:30 A.M., enter **7:30**. To set the clock to 7:30 P.M., enter **19:30**.

```
Current time is 12:23:39.82p
Enter new time: 19:30 <ENTER>
```

You can also use the letters A or P to indicate A.M. or P.M. For example, to enter the time 7:30 A.M., you can type **7:30A**. Likewise, to enter the time 7:30 P.M., you can type **7:30P**.

Next, your computer displays the characters **C>** (or something similar). These characters (usually followed by a blinking cursor) are called the *DOS prompt*. The prompt indicates the disk in use. **C>** indicates that the hard disk (drive C) is currently selected, whereas **A>** indicates that the floppy

Time	Military Hour	Time	Military Hour
12 P.M.	12	12 A.M.	00
1 P.M.	13	1 A.M.	01
2 P.M.	14	2 A.M.	02
3 P.M.	15	3 A.M.	03
4 P.M.	16	4 A.M.	04
5 P.M.	17	5 A.M.	05
6 P.M.	18	6 A.M.	06
7 P.M.	19	7 A.M.	07
8 P.M.	20	8 A.M.	08
9 P.M.	21	9 A.M.	09
10 P.M.	22	10 A.M.	10
11 P.M.	23	11 A.M.	11

Table 3-1. 24-hour Times

disk (drive A) is currently selected. In either case, the prompt indicates that DOS is successfully loaded, and the flashing cursor indicates it is ready to accept your commands.

```
Current date is Mon 04-05-1993
Enter new date (mm-dd-yy):

Current time is 12:23:39.82p
Enter new time:

Microsoft(R) MS-DOS(R)   Version 6.00
(C)Copyright Microsoft Corp 1981-1993

C>
```

If your computer is not displaying the DOS prompt or some other menu program from which you can run your necessary commands, use the trouble-shooting steps beginning on page 33. If your computer has successfully loaded DOS, Chapter 4 will teach you how to issue your first DOS commands.

System Startup

To start your computer and load DOS, following these steps:

Remove and store floppy
disks that may have been left
in a disk drive.

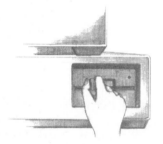

If you don't have DOS installed
on a hard disk, insert the System
Disk into drive A and close the
disk drive latch.

Make sure the computer, monitor,
and printer are plugged in and
turned on.

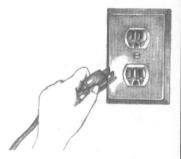

If the computer prompts you for a
new date or time, type the correct
date or time (or press ENTER to
leave the current settings
unchanged).

When DOS is successfully loaded, DOS will display its prompt
(typically **C>** or **A>**).

Troubleshooting

Several factors can keep your computer from successfully loading DOS. Read this section to quickly identify and correct such problems. (If you've had no problem loading DOS, you can skip to the next section.)

- Make sure your computer, monitor, and printer are each plugged into a working wall outlet.

- Make sure each piece of equipment is individually turned on. Make sure the monitor's intensity setting is not too dark or too light, so that you can clearly see messages displayed on the screen.

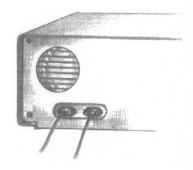

- Can you hear your computer's fan whirring? If not, your computer may have a power supply problem that requires maintenance by a hardware technician.

- Does your computer display its amount of RAM or any other messages on the screen during its initial testing? If not, your computer may be failing its self test, and will require maintenance by a hardware technician.

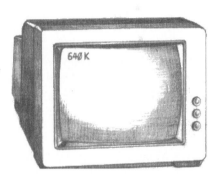

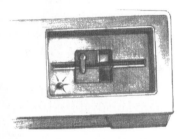

- Does your computer turn on the disk activation light? If not, your computer may be failing its self test, and will require maintenance by a hardware technician.

- Does your system display the message **Non-System disk or disk error**? If so, the computer cannot find DOS where it thinks it should be. If your computer uses a hard disk, remove any floppy disks from the disk drive, turn off your computer, then turn it on again. If the problem persists, DOS has not been correctly installed on your computer and you should turn to the installation notes that accompanied your computer. If your computer does not have a hard disk, place the DOS System Disk into drive A and restart your computer (turn it off and then back on).

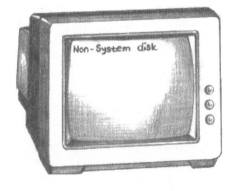

Keys to Success

To start up your computer, turn on the computer, monitor, and printer. The computer begins testing itself to make sure its components are in proper working order. After successfully completing its self test, the computer searches for DOS and begins loading it into RAM.

To help experienced users customize their systems, DOS allows users to specify one or more programs for automatic execution every time the system starts. Your automatic startup commands may differ from those on another user's computer, depending on how your system was installed. Some users may see a prompt for a new system date and time.

If you are prompted for a date and time, either press ENTER to accept the default date and time, or correct them and then press ENTER. Remember to use military (24-hour) time notation when entering the time.

When DOS is successfully loaded, you should eventually see the DOS prompt. For hard disk users, the prompt is normally the drive letter C followed by a greater-than symbol (**C>**). For floppy disk users, the DOS prompt uses the drive letter A (**A>**).

What Do They Mean by...?

A or C Prompt   Depending on your current disk drive, the DOS prompt typically displays as **A>** or **C>**. Users refer to these DOS prompts as the A prompt and C prompt.

Bootable Disk   A bootable disk is a system disk capable of starting DOS.

Booting DOS or Booting the Computer   The term *booting* means starting your computer. Because DOS is the first program your computer runs each time it starts, computer users often refer to this process as *booting DOS*.

System Disk   A system disk is a special disk that contains all the information the computer needs to load DOS. When you purchase DOS, one of the disks is labeled *DOS System Disk*. To start DOS from a floppy disk, insert the DOS System Disk into drive A. If this special DOS information has been copied to your hard disk, your hard disk becomes a system disk. A disk that does not contain the information necessary to load DOS is called a *non-system disk*.

Self Test   A self test is the internal checking done automatically by the computer when starting up. During the self test, your computer checks its hardware and software to make sure everything is working properly.

System Date and Time   Internally, your computer has a clock and calendar. These are used to regulate how the computer works. When you start your computer, you may have the opportunity to change the system date and time.

Typing In Your First DOS Commands

In Chapter 3 you learned how to turn on your computer and start DOS. After DOS successfully loads, it will display its prompt (usually **C>** on a system with a hard disk and **A>** on a system without a hard disk). Because most computers have hard disks, the examples in this chapter use the **C>** DOS prompt.

The DOS prompt indicates that DOS is ready to accept and execute your command. If you press the ENTER key several times without typing a command, DOS repeatedly displays its prompt and waits for you to enter a command name:

```
C> <ENTER>
C> <ENTER>
C>
```

If you type a command or program name before pressing the ENTER key, DOS attempts to execute a command, or to locate and run a program that matches the name you enter. DOS commands can contain up to eight characters. In many cases DOS uses an abbreviated name to reduce your typing. For example, the command name **CLS** (which causes DOS to clear the screen) is quick and easy to type. To execute this command, type the letters **CLS** at the DOS prompt and press ENTER:

```
C> CLS <ENTER>
```

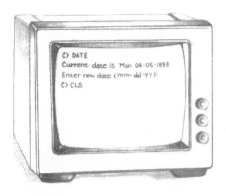

The DOS CLS command erases the screen's contents and redisplays the DOS prompt in the upper-left corner of the screen.

DOS responds to your command by clearing the screen and then redisplaying its prompt in the upper-left corner of the screen.

DOS does not distinguish between uppercase and lowercase letters. The following command also clears your screen:

```
C> cls <ENTER>
```

Correcting Typing Mistakes

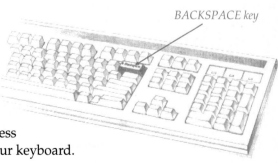

BACKSPACE key

If you type a wrong letter as you enter a command, locate and press the BACKSPACE key on your keyboard.

Pressing the BACKSPACE key erases the letter immediately to the left of the cursor. For example, assume that you mistype the CLS command as **CKS**. By pressing the BACKSPACE key twice, you can erase the letters S and K. You can then retype the correct command as shown here.

Using BACKSPACE to erase the letter S

Using BACKSPACE to erase the letter K

Correcting the command

Mistyping a Command and Pressing ENTER

When you type a command name and press the ENTER key, DOS checks to see if the command you have entered is in its list of frequently used commands. This group of DOS commands is referred to as *internal commands* because they are contained within (internal) the DOS program.

If DOS determines that the command is internal, it is executed immediately. If the command is *not* internal, DOS searches your disk for a file whose name matches the program name you have just entered. If a matching file is found, DOS loads the program from disk into memory and runs the program. If a matching file is *not* found, DOS displays a message indicating you have entered a bad command.

For example, enter the invalid command name **CKS** (a misspelling of CLS). DOS first searches for the command in memory. Because CKS is not an internal command, DOS next searches your disk for a file named CKS. (You should see your disk activation light illuminate briefly as DOS reads the disk and looks for this file.) When DOS fails to locate CKS on disk, it displays the error message shown here:

```
C> CKS <ENTER>
Bad command or file name
C>
```

After the error message, DOS redisplays its prompt to tell you it is ready for your next command. Type in the correct command and press ENTER to continue.

Running DOS Programs

To run a program from the DOS prompt, simply type the program name and press ENTER. DOS allows you to type the program name in either uppercase or lowercase letters. If you mistype a letter, the BACKSPACE key enables you to erase the letter immediately to the left of the cursor.

Each time you enter a program name, DOS first checks to see if the name corresponds to its list of internal commands. If a match is found, DOS executes the command. If no match is found, DOS searches the disk for a file name that matches the command you have entered. If a match is found, DOS loads the file into memory and runs it. If no matching file exists, DOS displays an error message.

More Simple Commands

This section discusses several more DOS commands. Rather than memorizing the commands, simply become familiar with typing (and possibly correcting) these commands.

Displaying the DOS Version Number

Programmers constantly work on new ways to make DOS faster and easier to use. Each time these programmers make a new version of the program available, they assign DOS a new version number. The VER command displays your DOS version number. To invoke the version command, type **VER** (an abbreviation for *version*) and press ENTER:

```
C> VER <ENTER>
```

DOS displays the version number of your program. VER is a simple command to run, and is easy to understand. Knowing how to use this command may help you when you have problems with your software.

You must know your DOS version number to know the specific operating system you are using. If you experience problems when you run a new software program, the manufacturer of that software will usually ask for your DOS version to make sure the program is designed to run under your version of DOS. In addition, some advanced DOS commands aren't included in all DOS versions. If you try to run such a command, DOS may display the "bad command" error message. Invoke VER now and note your DOS version.

Setting or Displaying the System Date

If your computer does not ask you to type in a new date each time it starts, you can display and, if necessary, change the current system date by using the DATE command. To run the DATE command, type **DATE** at the DOS prompt and press ENTER. DOS displays the current system date and prompts you to enter a new date:

```
C> DATE <ENTER>
Current date is Mon 04-05-1993
ENTER new date (mm-dd-yy):
```

You now can accept the default system date or enter a new one. If you are unsure of how to do this, you may want to refer back to Chapter 3.

If you mistype the date (such as by specifying an invalid date or by omitting the hyphens that separate the month, day, and year), DATE displays an error message and allows you to enter the date again:

```
C> DATE <ENTER>
Current date is Mon 04-05-1993
ENTER new date (mm-dd-yy): 7-14 <ENTER>
Invalid date
ENTER new date (mm-dd-yy): 7-14-93 <ENTER>
C>
```

Setting or Displaying the System Time

Just as the DATE command enables you to set or display the current system date, the TIME command enables you to set or display the current system time. Run this command by typing **TIME** and pressing ENTER. The TIME command displays the current system time and prompts you to enter a new time:

```
C> TIME <ENTER>
Current time is 12:23:39.82p
ENTER new time:
```

As with the DATE command, you can accept the default system time or enter a new one. If you are unsure of how to do this, you can refer back to Chapter 3.

If you enter an invalid time, DOS displays an error message and asks you to re-enter the system time. For example, the following command sets the current time to 2:30 P.M. (or 14:30 on a 24-hour clock):

```
C> TIME <ENTER>
Current time is 12:23:39.82p
ENTER new time: 14:30 <ENTER>
```

If you are using a version of DOS with a version number 4 or greater, the TIME command lets you append the letter A (for A.M.) or P (for P.M.) to the time instead of using the 24-hour military clock. Using the letter P, the following TIME command sets the system time to 2:30 P.M.:

```
C> TIME <ENTER>
Current time is 12:23:39.82p
ENTER new time: 2:30P <ENTER>
```

As discussed in Chapter 5, you must keep your system's date and time correctly set.

Additional Information for a Command

So far, each time you have run a DOS command, you have simply typed the command's name at the DOS prompt and pressed ENTER. Many of the programs you run may allow you to specify additional information on the command line. This may affect how the command functions. For example, you might be able to specify the desired system date when you invoke the DATE command. The following command sets the system date to December 25, 1993:

```
C> DATE 12-25-93
C>
```

Because the command specifies a date, there is no reason for DATE to prompt you for one. As a result, the system date is set to the date specified after the DATE command.

In the same way, the following TIME command sets the system time to 8:30 A.M.:

```
C> TIME 8:30
C>
```

You will include information after the command name for many of the commands you use throughout the rest of this book.

DOS Command Similarities

Although each of the DOS commands in this chapter seems simple, each illustrates the technique you use to execute every DOS command or program. Generally, you type in a command name at the DOS prompt, and possibly include a file name, a disk drive, or other command-line information. When DOS completes your command, it redisplays the DOS prompt and waits for you to type in your next command.

Providing Additional Command Information

The information you type at the DOS prompt before you press ENTER is called the *command line*. Many of the commands you issue in this book allow you to specify additional information in the command name. For example, the following DATE command includes the desired date in the command line.

C> DATE 12-08-93
C>

Because the command line includes the necessary date, the DATE command does not prompt you for one. Instead, DATE sets the system date to the date specified and returns to the DOS system prompt.

Learning to Understand DOS Error Messages

Many new DOS users are frustrated when they enter a command and, rather than running the program they expect, DOS displays an error message. For example, when you entered the invalid CKS command, DOS displayed the following:

```
C> CKS <ENTER>
Bad command or file name
C>
```

When an error message is displayed, take a few moments to try to understand the message. In this case, DOS is informing you that the information you entered is either a bad command or an invalid file name. Remember that when you enter a command name, DOS first checks to see if the name you type matches one of its internal commands. If not, it looks for a disk file whose name matches the command. If a match still can't be found, it tells you that you have typed in a bad command (one that does not match an internal command name) or file name (one that does not match a program file name on disk).

One of the most common causes of this error message is misspelling the command name. If you are sure the program name is spelled correctly, make sure you are using the correct subdirectory for the command. Chapter 6 explains DOS subdirectories in detail.

Cancelling a DOS Command

As you work with DOS, you may enter a DOS command or an application program command and realize you really don't want to execute the command. In most cases, you can end commands by holding down the CTRL key and pressing C.

Pressing two or more keys at the same time is referred to as a *keyboard combination.* In this case, to cancel a command, you will use the CTRL-C keyboard combination. Many books, including as
the DOS user's manual, illustrate keyboard combinations by placing a plus sign between the keys involved. In this case, the keyboard combination becomes CTRL+C. You don't type the plus character, but rather hold down the CTRL key and then press C.

For example, in-
voke the DATE com-
mand. DATE will dis-
play the current
system date and
prompt you to enter a
new date:

```
C> DATE <ENTER>
Current date is Mon 04-05-1993
ENTER new date (mm-dd-yy):
```

Rather than entering a new date, press CTRL-C to terminate the command. As you do, DOS displays the characters **^C** on your screen, terminates the command, and redisplays the DOS prompt:

```
C> DATE <ENTER>
Current date is Mon 04-05-1993
ENTER new date (mm-dd-yy): ^C
C>
```

Keys to Success

To execute a program, type the program's name in either uppercase or lowercase letters at the DOS prompt, and press ENTER. If DOS locates the command in memory or as a file on your disk, DOS runs the program. If DOS fails to locate a matching command or file, it displays a "bad command or file name" error message.

If you mistype a command name, and have not yet pressed ENTER, you can correct the command using your keyboard's BACKSPACE key. BACKSPACE erases the letter immediately to the left of the cursor.

Many commands allow you to type additional information after the command name (before you press ENTER) to run the command.

What Do They Mean by...?

Command Line   When you type a command name at the DOS prompt, the command name and information you type after the name comprise your command line.

External Command   An external command is a program that resides as a file on disk. When you execute an external command, DOS must load the program from disk into electronic memory before the command can be executed. All applications programs (such as word processors or spreadsheets) are executed with external commands.

Internal Command   An internal command is a frequently used DOS command (such as CLS, DATE, and TIME) that DOS stores in your computer's electronic memory. By keeping the internal command in memory (as opposed to having to first load the command from disk), DOS can execute the command much faster.

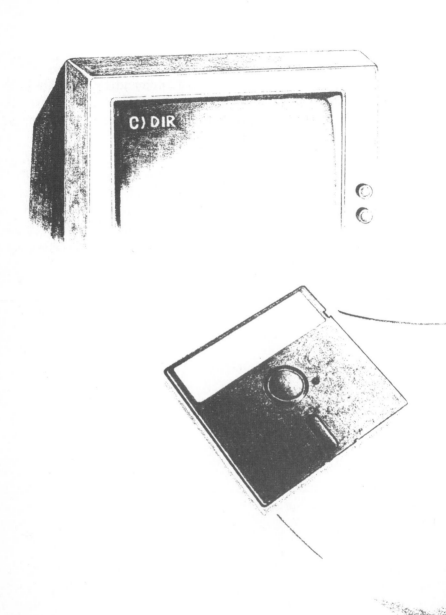

Listing Your Files Stored on Disk

5

Interruptions are a fact of everyday life and can disrupt your computer work. You may have to start and stop your work on letters, reports, and other documents you generate using your computer. Your document information can be safely stored on your computer's disk between work sessions. Just as you may physically place related information in a paper file folder, DOS stores related information in files on your disk. In fact, DOS keeps all the information on your disk stored in a series of individual files.

Listing the Files on Your Disk

One of the most common activities you will perform on your computer is searching your disk for specific files. To help you organize your disk, DOS lets you group files into lists or areas called *directories*. The DIR (short for *directory*) command lets you display the name of each file in a disk's directory. To view the files in your directory, type **DIR** and press ENTER. Using the directory that contains your DOS files as an example, DIR displays the name, the size, and the date and time each file was created or modified. Issuing the DIR command for that directory results in something similar to the following:

```
C:\DOS> DIR  <ENTER>

 Volume in drive C has no label
 Volume Serial Number is 1A43-5E8B
 Directory of C:\DOS

      .            <DIR>      11-23-92    9:26p
      . .          <DIR>      11-23-92    9:26p
 EGA       SYS      4885 01-28-93    6:00a
 FORMAT    COM     22717 01-28-93    6:00a
 NLSFUNC   EXE      7036 01-28-93    6:00a
 COUNTRY   SYS     17066 01-28-93    6:00a
 EGA       CPI     58870 01-28-93    6:00a
 HIMEM     SYS     14160 01-28-93    6:00a
 KEYB      COM     14983 01-28-93    6:00a
 KEYBOARD  SYS     34694 01-28-93    6:00a
```

```
ANSI      SYS      9065 01-28-93    6:00a
ATTRIB    EXE     11165 01-28-93    6:00a
  :        :        :     :          :
DELTREE   EXE      9603 01-28-93    6:00a
INTERLNK  EXE     17133 01-28-93    6:00a
INTERSVR  EXE     37266 01-28-93    6:00a
MOVE      EXE     17091 01-28-93    6:00a
SMARTDRV  EXE     42073 01-28-93    6:00a
         nn file(s)    7527422 bytes
                       9166848 bytes free
```

You might think of DIR as listing the name of every file in a filing cabinet drawer.

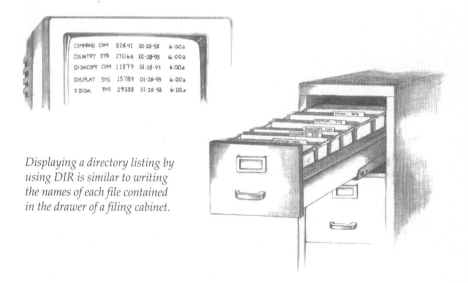

Displaying a directory listing by using DIR is similar to writing the names of each file contained in the drawer of a filing cabinet.

Every file in a directory has a unique file name. A DOS file name consists of two parts: an eight-character base name, and a three-character extension. For example, in the file name SMARTDRV.SYS, the base name is SMARTDRV, and the extension is SYS. The base name helps you determine the contents of the file, while the extension identifies the type of the file.

You should know a few hard and fast rules about base names and extensions. First, for files you create, you determine the file name yourself.

For files containing letters, for example, you may use the extension LTR. Likewise, for files containing reports, you might use the extension RPT.

Next, when you create a file name, you use a period to separate the base name from the extension. By combining a descriptive file name with a meaningful extension, you produce names that make it very easy to determine the contents of a file. Table 5-1 combines descriptive file names and extensions to create several meaningful examples.

DOS Files

Every piece of information you store on your disk must reside in a file. DOS organizes files by grouping them into lists called directories. A directory is similar to a filing cabinet drawer. Every file in a directory must have a unique name. A DOS file name consists of two parts: an eight-character base name and a three-character extension. The DIR command displays the name, size, and creation date and time for each file in a directory.

Not every base name uses all eight possible character positions. However, if you use fewer than eight characters, you may find it difficult to create a descriptive name.

As you examine the files on your disk, you may find files with the extensions EXE, COM, BAT, or SYS. These file extensions typically correspond to DOS commands and other application programs. Table 5-2 briefly summarizes these commonly used extensions.

Filename.Ext	File's Contents
BUDGET93.RPT	Report on the 1993 budget
CREDIT.LTR	Letter to a credit department
SALESOCT.MEM	Memo about October sales

Table 5-1. Meaningful File Names and Extensions

Extension	File's Contents
EXE or COM	A program DOS can run. You can instruct DOS to run the program by typing the base name at the DOS prompt.
BAT	A batch file, which is simply a file containing a list of DOS commands. You can execute all of the commands in the list by typing the base name for the batch file at the DOS prompt.
SYS	A special operating system file possibly used by DOS during system startup.

Table 5-2. Meaningful File Names and Extensions

More About DIR

As mentioned, a directory of files on your disk is similar to a filing cabinet drawer filled with files. Like the drawers of a filing cabinet, the directories on your disk exist to help you organize your files. As you store new programs on your disk, you will create many different directories, each with its own unique name. For now, think of a directory as simply a list of files.

If you are using a hard disk, your DOS files may reside in a directory named DOS. To view the names of the files in this directory, invoke DIR and include the directory name \DOS in your command line:

```
C> DIR \DOS <ENTER>
```

Make sure you type the backslash before the name DOS. What you have done is to instruct DOS to display the directory for only a limited part of your hard disk—for one subdirectory. In this case, you have specified that DIR should display the names of each file in the DOS subdirectory.

Depending on the number of files in your DOS directory, the file names may scroll up the screen too quickly to be read. If this occurs, include the

/P qualifier in the DIR command line to direct DIR to pause with each screenful of filenames.

```
C> DIR \DOS /P <ENTER>
```

Note the opposite directions of the slashes. A backslash precedes the directory (\DOS), while a regular slash precedes the qualifier (/P).

Understanding File Sizes

As discussed in Chapter 1, DOS expresses the size of your files in bytes. (Remember, a byte is equivalent to about one character.) A file that is 50 bytes in length, for example, contains 50 characters. A single-spaced typed page, for example, requires about 4000 bytes. The DIR command displays the size of each file in a directory.

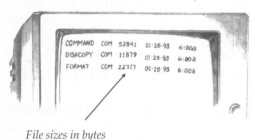

File sizes in bytes

DIR displays the size of each file in bytes

In addition to the size of each file, the last two lines that DIR displays indicate the number of files in the directory listing, the disk space that the listed files consume, and the amount of free space on your disk. This disk space information is also provided in bytes.

DIR always displays the amount of available disk space, as well as the number of files displayed in the listing and the disk space the files consume.

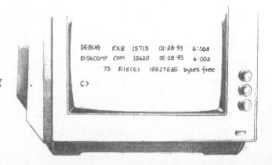

Understanding the Date and Time Stamp

Each time you create a new file or change the contents of an existing file, DOS records the current system date and time in the file's directory entry. By using DIR to display the directory information, you can view the date and time stamp of each file and determine when the file was created or last changed.

If your computer's current system date and time is incorrect, DOS will assign the wrong date and time stamp to every file you create or change. Use the DATE and TIME commands discussed in Chapters 3 and 4 to be sure your system date and time are correct.

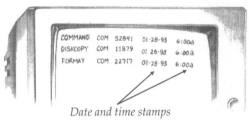

Date and time stamps

DIR displays the date and time stamp of each file, which tells you when the file was created or when it was last changed.

Displaying Files on Another Disk

Every disk drive on your computer has a unique corresponding drive letter. A hard disk, for example, is normally drive C. Floppy disks normally are assigned the drive letters A and B.

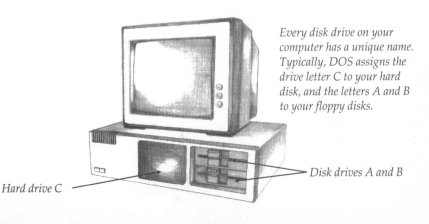

Every disk drive on your computer has a unique name. Typically, DOS assigns the drive letter C to your hard disk, and the letters A and B to your floppy disks.

Disk drives A and B

Hard drive C

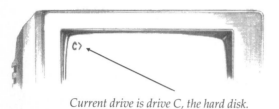

Current drive is drive C, the hard disk.

The DOS prompt typically displays the drive letter of the current drive.

You can select one of your disk drives as the drive in which DOS automatically searches for programs when you type in a program name at the DOS prompt. DOS calls this drive the *default drive*. The DOS prompt normally contains the drive letter of the default drive.

To change default drives, type the letter of the desired drive, immediately follow that letter with a colon (:), and press ENTER. DOS acknowledges the change in drives by immediately changing the letter that appears at the DOS prompt. For example, the following command changes the default drive from drive C to drive A:

```
C> A: <ENTER>
A>
```

If you issue the DIR command after changing the default drive to A, DIR displays the name of each file on the disk in drive A. Now change the default drive back to C:

```
A> C: <ENTER>
C>
```

The default drive is so named because, by default, it is where DOS performs its disk-related operations (such as searching for files or disk-based commands).

Using Different Disk Drives

Every disk drive has a unique single-letter name. The hard disk is normally drive C. Your floppy disks are drive A and drive B. The current drive, or *default* drive, is the disk drive DOS uses, by default, in its operations. The DOS prompt normally contains the letter of the default drive.

To change the default drive, type the letter of the desired drive followed by a colon and press ENTER.

The DIR command displays the names of the files in a directory. To display the names of files that reside on another disk, issue the DIR command and type the drive letter of the desired disk followed by a colon.

So far you have only used DIR to display files that reside on the current drive. In many cases, you may need to examine the names of files that reside on a floppy disk. To do so, you still use the DIR command. However, in this case you specify the letter of the desired disk drive (followed by a colon) immediately after the DIR command. For example, the following command directs DIR to display the files that reside on the disk in drive A:

```
C> DIR A: <ENTER>
```

If your disk is in drive B, you can view the names of files on that drive by using B:

```
C> DIR B: <ENTER>
```

Understanding the "Abort, Retry, Fail?" Error Message

Users working with floppy disks often commit two common errors: failing to close the disk drive's latch, and inserting a floppy disk that has not yet been prepared for use by DOS. When one of these conditions occurs, DOS displays a message that indicates the cause of the error, along with the following prompt:

```
Abort, Retry, Fail?
```

This is displayed when DOS encounters a condition from which it cannot recover without your help. In this case, DOS gives you three choices. First, you can abort (or end) the operation by typing the letter **A**.

If you know how to correct the error (by closing the disk drive latch, for instance), do so, and then type **R** to retry the operation.

In rare cases, DOS may experience an error when attempting to read from a disk. Typing **F** for the Fail option instructs DOS to ignore this error and attempt to continue executing the command. Periodically, you can use the Fail option to copy files from a partially damaged disk.

To better understand this error message, select your hard disk (drive C) as the current default. Next, open the disk drive latch for drive A and remove any floppy disk in the drive. Then use the DIR command to display the directory for drive A. Because drive A does not contain a disk, DOS issues an error message. You should then type **A** to abort the DIR command. DOS returns to the DOS prompt:

```
C> DIR A: <ENTER>
Not ready reading drive A
Abort, Retry, Fail? A

C>
```

Abort, Retry, Fail?

Periodically, DOS encounters an error (such as an open disk drive latch or a printer with no paper) that prevents it from continuing without your intervention. When such an error occurs, DOS displays a message explaining the cause of the error, followed by a prompt to Abort, Retry, or Fail the current command. When DOS displays this message, it expects you to type the letter A, R, or F (Abort, Retry, or Fail).

The Abort option directs DOS to end the current command that is causing the error. If you select Abort, DOS returns control to the DOS prompt.

If you know how to correct the error, do so and type **R**. The Retry option directs DOS to repeat the operation.

Repeat the DIR command. This time, when DOS displays the error message, place a floppy disk in the disk drive and close the disk drive latch. Type **R** to retry the operation. Because drive A now contains a disk, the command executes and DIR displays the names of the files that reside in that directory.

Sorting Your Directory Listing

Unless you tell it to do otherwise, DIR displays its list of files in the same order in which the files appear in the directory list. When you search for a file, there may be times when it is convenient to view a directory list sorted by name, extension, size, or date. If you are using DOS 5 or later, DIR lets you display a sorted directory listing. For example, if you include the command-line switch /O:N, the following DIR command displays a sorted directory listing:

```
C:\DOS> DIR /O:N  <ENTER>

Volume in drive C has no label
Volume Serial Number is 1A43-5E8B
Directory of C:\DOS

.                   <DIR>      11-23-92    9:26p
..                  <DIR>      11-23-92    9:26p
ANSI      SYS        9065  01-28-93    6:00a
APPEND    EXE       10774  01-28-93    6:00a
APPNOTES  TXT        9058  12-06-92    6:00a
ATTRIB    EXE       11165  01-28-93    6:00a
CHKDSK    EXE       12908  01-28-93    6:00a
CHKLIST   CPS        2727  01-26-93    2:28p
CHOICE    COM        1754  01-28-93    6:00a
   :        :          :       :          :
TREE      COM        6898  01-28-93    6:00a
UNDELETE  EXE       26420  01-28-93    6:00a
UNFORMAT  COM       12738  01-28-93    6:00a
XCOPY     EXE       15820  01-28-93    6:00a
         nn file(s)      7527422 bytes
                         9164800 bytes free
```

Table 5-3 lists the command-line switches you should use to sort your directories using different formats. DIR actually provides you with even greater control of your directory listings than discussed here. As you become more comfortable with DOS, issue the command DIR /? to learn more about DIR's capabilities.

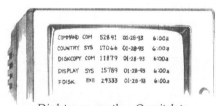

Dir lets you use the =O switch to display sorted directory listings.

DIR Command	Directory Listing
DIR /O:N	Sorted by name from A through Z
DIR /O:E	Sorted by extension from A through Z
DIR /O:S	Sorted by size from smallest to largest
DIR /O:D	Sorted by date from oldest to newest
DIR /O:G	Directory names before file names
DIR /O:C	Sorted by compression ratio (DOS 6)

Table 5-3. DOS 5 and 6 DIR Sort Options

Keys to Success

To store information on your disk between computer sessions, you must place the information in a file. To organize your disks, DOS lets you group related files into lists called directories. This process is similar to grouping related files in a filing cabinet drawer.

Every file in a directory must have a unique name. A DOS file name consists of two parts: an eight-character base name and a three-character extension. The base name gives specific information about the actual file, while the extension specifies what type of file it is. The DIR command displays a list of files in a directory. It displays each file's name, extension, size, and the date and time the file was created (or last changed).

Every disk drive in your computer has a unique single-letter name. A hard disk, for example, is named drive C. Floppy disks are typically named A and B. One of your disks is the default drive that DOS uses for its operations. To change the default drive, at the DOS prompt type the letter of the desired drive, followed by a colon, and press ENTER.

What Do They Mean by...?

Default Disk Drive   Most computers have a hard disk and one or more floppy disk drives. When you work with your computer, DOS allows you to select one of the disk drives as the drive in which it searches for files and commands unless you explicitly tell it to look elsewhere. The DOS prompt typically displays the letter of the current default drive.

Directory   To organize the files stored on your disk, DOS groups the files into lists called directories. A directory is similar to a drawer of a filing cabinet. As you purchase different software programs, you will create individual directories to store each program's files.

File Extension   A DOS file name has two parts: an eight-character base name and a three-character extension. The extension is used to specify the file's type, such as a letter (LTR), report (RPT), or memo (MEM). By combining a descriptive base name with an extension, you can describe a file's contents.

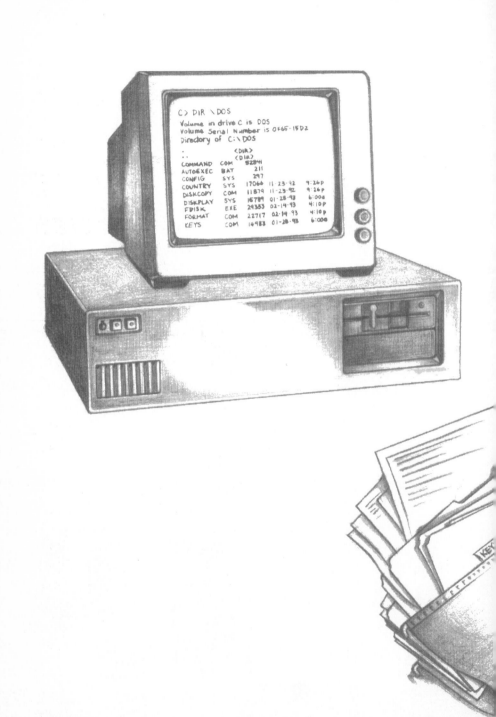

Creating Your Own Directories to Organize Your Files

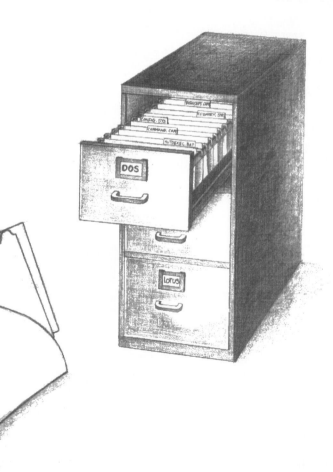

As discussed in Chapter 5, a directory on your disk is much like a drawer containing one or more files in a filing cabinet. Just as you would use a filing cabinet to organize your paper files, you should create directories on your disk to organize files. The DIR command displays the names of files that reside in a specific directory. To help you work with directories, DOS provides the following three important commands:

CHDIR	Used to change the current directory
MKDIR	Used to create a directory
RMDIR	Used to remove an empty directory from your disk

Building a Foundation

All DOS disks begin with one directory called the *root directory*, or simply the *root*. The root directory is so named because all the directories you will later create grow out of the root directory, much like the branches of a tree originally start at the tree's root. DOS uses the backslash character (\) to represent the root. This character represents the name of the root directory and cannot be changed.

Initially, your hard disk only contains the root directory and no others, much like an empty filing cabinet.

Initially, the only directory on your disk is the root directory. The empty root directory is much like an empty filing cabinet waiting to hold files.

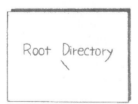

When you install DOS on your hard disk, you create a directory named DOS, and store within that directory all of the DOS files.

Creating the DOS
subdirectory on your
disk is similar to
labeling a drawer of
a filing cabinet.

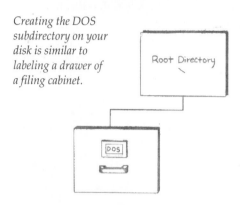

As you later purchase additional software programs (such as a word processor and spreadsheet), you must create a directory for each one. You store within each application's directory the corresponding program and its files. Assume, for example, that you are installing the WordPerfect word processor and the Lotus 1-2-3 spreadsheet program. You could create the directories WP and LOTUS.

Adding the WP and LOTUS directories to your disk
essentially labels two more file cabinet drawers.

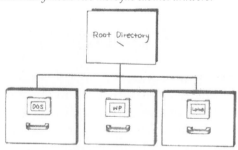

As you work with your word processor, you may soon find that your many letters and reports make it difficult to locate files within the directory for the word processing program. You can create additional levels of directories to improve your file organization, much as you would place dividers in a drawer of the filing cabinet.

As you can see, your disk's subdirectories soon begin to resemble a tree with several branches that have grown from the root. The longer you work with DOS, the more directories your disk will contain. When you issue the DIR command, DIR displays the entries for files in a specific directory.

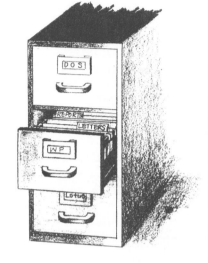

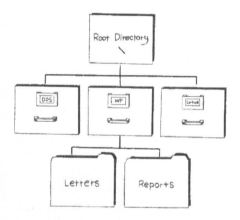

Creating additional directories on your disk beneath WP is similar to placing dividers within the filing cabinet drawer labeled WP.

Selecting the Default Directory

Although your disk may contain many directories, DOS lets you select one directory as the current (or *default*) directory. The current directory contains those files DOS uses to perform actions, unless you explicitly tell it to act otherwise. The current directory is your disk's counterpart to an open drawer of a filing cabinet, or a specific divider within the drawer.

Remember, the DOS prompt typically contains the drive letter of the current drive. The following PROMPT command directs DOS to display the current drive and the current directory within the prompt. Using this command helps simplify changing from one directory to another.

```
C> PROMPT   $P$G <Enter>
C:\>
```

The prompt now tells you the current drive is drive C (C:) and the current directory is the root (the \ symbol).

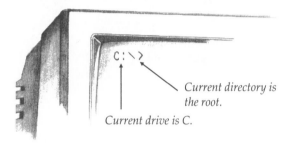

Current directory is the root.

Current drive is C.

The CHDIR command lets you change from one directory to another. Changing the current directory is much like closing one drawer of a filing cabinet and opening another. For example, the following command changes the current directory to the DOS directory. When you press ENTER, notice that DOS has updated your system prompt to indicate the directory change.

```
C:\> CHDIR \DOS <ENTER>
C:\DOS>
```

In this example, selecting the DOS directory is similar to opening the filing cabinet drawer labeled DOS.

C:\ > CHDIR\DOS

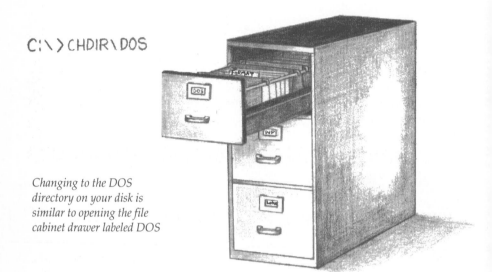

*Changing to the DOS
directory on your disk is
similar to opening the file
cabinet drawer labeled DOS*

Virtually any DOS command will affect only the files within the current directory. To continue this example, if you now use the DIR command, only the files within the DOS directory are listed.

To change from the DOS directory back to the root, use CHDIR with the root directory symbol (\).

```
C:\DOS> CHDIR \ <ENTER>
C:\>
```

By using the CHDIR command, you can select any directory on your disk as the current directory.

In order to create a few more directories with which to experiment, you will learn next how to make your own directories by using the MKDIR command.

The CHDIR Command

To organize your files on disk, DOS lets you create lists of files called directories. A directory is similar to a drawer of a filing cabinet. The CHDIR command lets you change from one directory to another. Changing directories is conceptually similar to closing one drawer of a filing cabinet and opening another.

Creating Your Own Directories

Each time you purchase a new software program, you should create a new directory on your hard disk in which to store the program's files. (The installation procedure of most software packages handles this task for you.) Or, you might have too many files in one directory and have difficulty locating certain files. In this case, you should create one or more additional directories to improve your file organization.

The MKDIR command lets you create additional directories on your hard disk. Creating a directory is similar to assigning a name to a drawer of a filing cabinet, or adding a divider within a drawer of existing files to improve your organization.

For this example, be sure you are at the root directory and then use MKDIR to create the directory TESTDIR:

```
C:\> MKDIR TESTDIR <ENTER>
```

Issue the DIR command and a directory listing of the root directory reveals that the new directory TESTDIR has been created.

```
C:\> DIR  <ENTER>

  Volume in drive C has no label
  Volume Serial Number is 1A43-5E8B
  Directory of C:\

COMMAND  COM     52841 01-28-93    6:00a
DOS          <DIR>      02-15-93    1:59p
AUTOEXEC BAT       211 02-14-93    4:10p
CONFIG   SYS       297 02-14-93    4:10p
TESTDIR      <DIR>      02-15-93    2:00p
        5 file(s)        53349 bytes
                       9277440 bytes free
```

Your directory listing probably differs (you may have many, many more files). However, if you correctly issued the command, TESTDIR should be somewhere within the list of files now displayed. Note that the word <DIR> appears after the names of directories on your disk. This helps distinguish directories from regular files when the list is displayed. Use the CHDIR command to select TESTDIR as the current directory.

```
C:\> CHDIR TESTDIR <ENTER>
C:\TESTDIR>
```

A directory listing of TESTDIR reveals the following:

```
C:\TESTDIR> DIR  <ENTER>

  Volume in drive C has no label
  Volume Serial Number is 1A43-5E8B
  Directory of C:\TESTDIR

   .         <DIR>      02-15-93    1:29p
   ..        <DIR>      02-15-93    1:29p
        2 file(s)            0 bytes
                       9332736 bytes free
```

Notice that two new directories are listed for the directory you just created! Every directory you create will automatically have these two special directory entries (. and ..). As you become more conversant with DOS, you will use these two entries as abbreviations in your directory commands. For now, however, simply realize that DOS automatically places these entries in every directory you create.

Also notice that this listing shows the name of the current drive as well as the directory. In this example, DIR displays the drive letter C and the directory name TESTDIR.

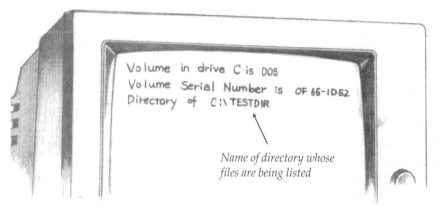

Name of directory whose files are being listed

DIR always displays the name of the directory whose files it is listing.

Use the following MKDIR command to create the subdirectory ONE within the directory TESTDIR.

```
C:\TESTDIR> MKDIR ONE <ENTER>
```

Note that ONE is not preceded with the backslash character, as in previous examples. When you don't precede a directory name with a backslash, MKDIR creates a new *subdirectory* within the current directory. This is similar to placing a divider labeled ONE within the filing cabinet drawer labeled TESTDIR.

C:\ TESTDIR > MKDIR ONE < Enter >

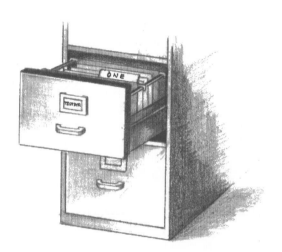

Creating the directory ONE within TESTDIR is similar to inserting a divider labeled one in a filing cabinet drawer labeled TESTDIR.

A directory listing of TESTDIR reveals that MKDIR has created the subdirectory ONE within TESTDIR.

```
C:\TESTDIR> DIR   <ENTER>

Volume in drive C has no label
Volume Serial Number is 1A43-5E8B
Directory of C:\TESTDIR

.               <DIR>      02-15-93    1:29p
..              <DIR>      02-15-93    1:29p
ONE             <DIR>      02-15-93    2:03p
       3 file(s)             0 bytes
                       9332736 bytes free
```

Use CHDIR to select the subdirectory ONE as the current directory.

```
C:\TESTDIR> CHDIR ONE <ENTER>
C:\TESTDIR\ONE>
```

The biggest step you must climb when working with DOS directories and subdirectories is learning when to precede a directory name with a backslash and when not to use the backslash. Remember, if the subdirectory you want to create (or want to change to) resides immediately below the current directory, don't include the backslash.

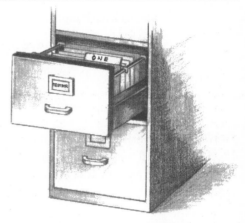

Current directory

For example, the current directory (and subdirectory) is TESTDIR\ONE.

When you try to select the DOS directory as the current directory without including a backslash, the CHDIR command fails and the command results in an error message. You then retain TESTDIR\ONE as the current directory.

Selecting the directory ONE as the current directory on your disk is similar to looking at the files stored in the divider labeled ONE.

```
C:\TESTDIR\ONE> CHDIR DOS  <ENTER>
Invalid directory
C:\TESTDIR\ONE>
```

The only time you don't precede the directory name with a backslash is when the area you want to select resides below (within) the current directory (a subdirectory). Because the DOS directory does not reside below the subdirectory ONE (but rather immediately below the root directory), you must specify the backslash before the DOS directory name, as shown here:

```
C:\TESTDIR\ONE> CHDIR \DOS <ENTER>
C:\DOS>
```

When you specify a directory name, think of the name as providing DOS with a road map to use when locating that directory.

For example, assume that your disk contains the following directories (and subdirectory), and that the current directory is DOS.

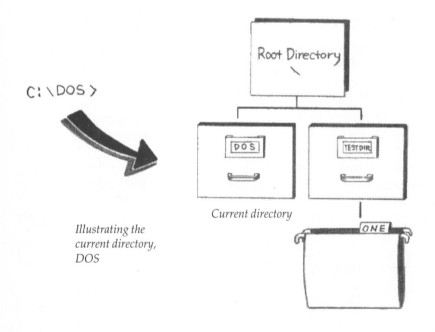

Current directory

Illustrating the current directory, DOS

Now assume you want to select the directory TESTDIR. You must tell DOS to begin at the root directory (\) and then select TESTDIR (which resides below the root).

`C:\DOS> CHDIR \TESTDIR <Enter>`

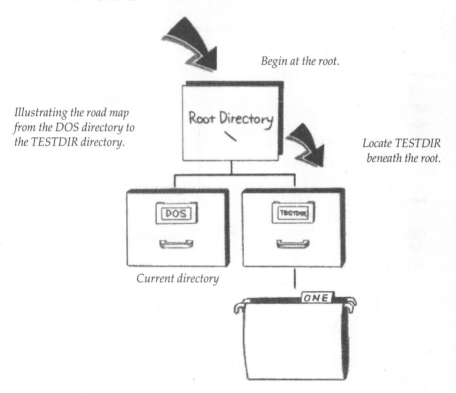

Begin at the root.

Illustrating the road map from the DOS directory to the TESTDIR directory.

Locate TESTDIR beneath the root.

Current directory

To change to the subdirectory TESTDIR\ONE from the directory DOS, you must tell CHDIR to begin at the root directory (\), locate TESTDIR, and then locate the subdirectory ONE within the TESTDIR directory, as shown next.

C:\DOS> CHDIR \TESTDIR\ONE   <Enter>

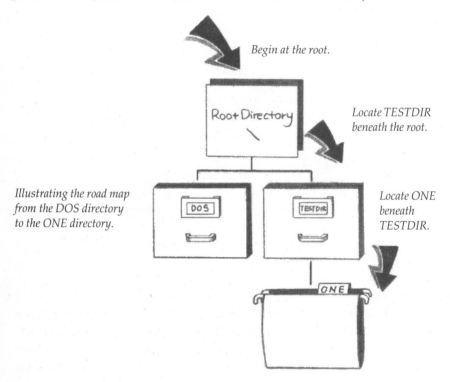

Begin at the root.

Locate TESTDIR beneath the root.

Illustrating the road map from the DOS directory to the ONE directory.

Locate ONE beneath TESTDIR.

If the current directory is TESTDIR, and you want to change to the subdirectory ONE, your road map is much simpler.

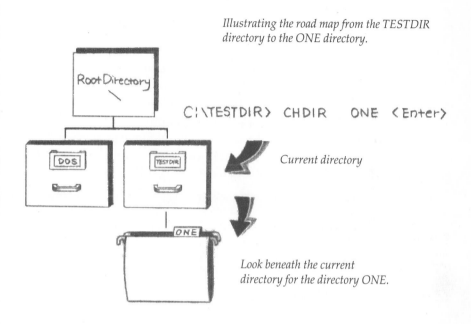

Illustrating the road map from the TESTDIR directory to the ONE directory.

C:\TESTDIR> CHDIR   ONE <Enter>

Current directory

Look beneath the current directory for the directory ONE.

If you precede the subdirectory name ONE with a slash (\ONE), your road map tells DOS to begin at the root and to search for the directory ONE. Because the subdirectory ONE does not reside immediately below the root, the command fails and DOS displays an "invalid directory" error message.

```
C:\TESTDIR> CHDIR \ONE   <Enter>
Invalid directory
C:\TESTDIR>
```

If you issue DOS commands that can't locate a specific directory, make sure you are specifying a complete road map (called a directory path) that DOS can follow to locate that directory.

The MKDIR Command

The MKDIR command lets you create your own directories to improve your file organization. Creating a subdirectory on your disk is much like labeling a filing cabinet, or adding a divider to a drawer of files, to improve your file organization.

As the number of files in a directory becomes difficult to manage, use MKDIR to further divide your directories into additional sub-directories to improve your file organization.

Removing Unused Directories with RMDIR

Just as the MKDIR command improves your file organization by enabling you to make a directory, the RMDIR command lets you remove an empty directory that is no longer needed. Removing a directory from your disk is similar to removing a divider from a filing cabinet drawer, or to removing the label from the drawer itself.

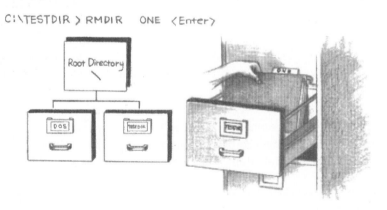

Removing the directory ONE from the TESTDIR directory is similar to removing the divider labeled ONE from a filing cabinet drawer.

For example, use CHDIR to change to the directory TESTDIR. Next, use the following RMDIR command to remove the subdirectory ONE.

```
C:\TESTDIR> RMDIR ONE <ENTER>
```

A directory listing of your TESTDIR directory reveals that the directory ONE has been successfully removed.

```
C:\TESTDIR> DIR   <ENTER>

 Volume in drive C has no label
 Volume Serial Number is 1A43-5E8B
 Directory of C:\TESTDIR

 .              <DIR>       02-15-93    1:29p
 ..             <DIR>       02-15-93    1:29p
        2 file(s)               0 bytes
                        9332736 bytes free
```

The RMDIR command only allows you to remove an empty directory. If you try to remove a directory containing files, the RMDIR command results in an error message that tells you the directory contains files, and then the command fails.

Likewise, RMDIR does not allow you to remove the current directory. If you try to use RMDIR to remove the current directory TESTDIR, the command fails, as shown here:

```
C:\TESTDIR> RMDIR \TESTDIR
Attempt to remove current directory - \TESTDIR
C:\TESTDIR>
```

The RMDIR Command

The RMDIR command lets you remove an empty directory from your disk when the directory is no longer needed. This is similar to removing the label from a filing cabinet drawer, or removing an empty divider from within a drawer of files.

The RMDIR command only lets you remove empty directories— ones that don't contain any files or subdirectories. In addition, this command does not allow you to remove the current directory.

To remove the directory TESTDIR from your disk, you must first change to a different directory. In this case, change to the directory DOS and then use RMDIR (including a complete path name) to remove TESTDIR:

```
C:\TESTDIR> CHDIR \DOS <ENTER>
C:\DOS>
C:\DOS> RMDIR \TESTDIR <ENTER>
```

Note: If you are using DOS 6, the DELTREE command lets you delete a directory, along with all the files and subdirectories it contains, in one easy step.

Abbreviating Directory Commands

The DOS directory manipulation commands MKDIR, CHDIR, and RMDIR are three of the most commonly used DOS commands. To save keystrokes when you use these commands, DOS allows you to abbreviate them as simply MD (for make directory), CD (for change directory), and RD (for remove directory). For example, the following command uses CD to change to the root directory.

```
C:\DOS> CD \ <ENTER>
C:\>
```

Keys to Success

A directory is a list of files on your disk. To help organize your files, DOS allows you to create directories. Creating a directory on your disk is similar to labeling a drawer of a filing cabinet (or placing a divider within an existing drawer of files) to improve your file organization.

Every DOS disk begins with one directory called the *root directory*. DOS uses the backslash symbol (\) to represent the root.

The CHDIR command lets you change the current directory. It can be abbreviated as CD. Selecting a directory with CHDIR is similar to opening a specific filing cabinet drawer, or accessing a divider full of files within the drawer.

The MKDIR command lets you make a directory. Because you will use MKDIR often, DOS lets you abbreviate it as simply MD.

The RMDIR command lets you remove a directory from your disk when it is no longer needed. It can be abbreviated as RD. Removing a directory is equivalent to removing an unused divider from a filing cabinet drawer, or removing the label from the filing cabinet drawer when the drawer no longer contains files. The RMDIR command only lets you remove empty directories. You cannot remove the current directory.

What Do They Mean by...?

Default Directory   The default directory is another name for the current directory. The CHDIR command lets you change the current, or default, directory.

Directory Tree   The directory tree contains all the directories on your disk, beginning with the root directory.

Parent Directory   The parent directory is the directory immediately above the current directory. The root directory, for example, is the parent directory for \DOS. Likewise, the directory \TESTDIR is the parent directory for the subdirectory \TESTDIR\ONE.

Empty Directory   An empty directory is a directory that contains no files or directories.

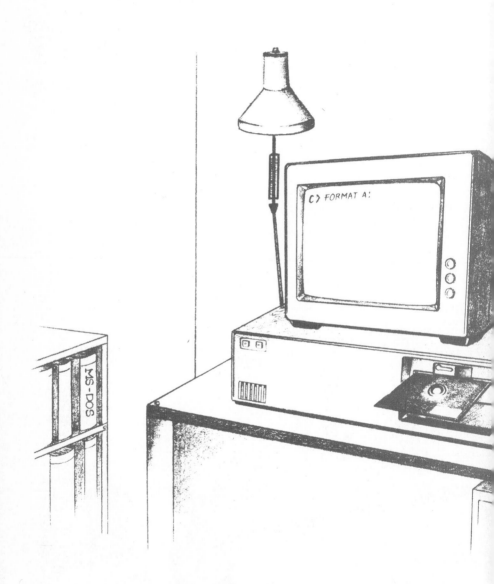

Preparing a Disk for Use by DOS

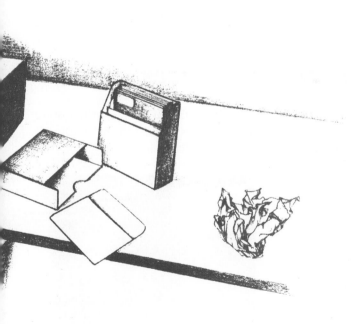

Each time you purchase a box of floppy disks, you must prepare the disks by using the FORMAT command. Until you format (or prepare) a disk for use, DOS cannot store files on the disk. Here's why. When a disk is made, the manufacturer has no way of knowing if you intend to use the disk on an Apple computer, an IBM PC, or any other computer. Because of this, the disk manufacturer lets you prepare a disk for use on a specific computer. If you attempt to access a disk that has not yet been formatted, DOS displays the following error message.

```
General failure reading drive A
Abort, Retry, Fail?
```

The process of preparing a disk for use is called *disk formatting.*

Understanding Disk Sizes

Formatting disks is one of the few times you will need to pay attention to the amount of data a floppy disk can store. As discussed in Chapter 1, floppy disks come in two sizes: 3 1/2 inch and 5 1/4 inch.

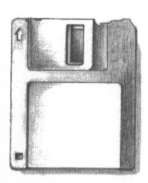

Name	Characteristics	Storage Capacity
360KB	Double-sided, double-density	368,640 bytes
1.2MB	Double-sided, quad-density	1,213,952 bytes

Table 7-1. Common 5 1/4-Inch Disk Types

However, even though two disks may be the same physical size, they may not be capable of storing the same amount of information. The difference in disk storage capability is due to advances in technology. Today, the most common 5 1/4-inch disks store either 360KB or 1.2MB of information. Table 7-1 describes the two most common 5 1/4-inch disks. The most common 3 1/2-inch disks can store 720KB, 1.44MB, or 2.88MB. Table 7-2 describes these 3 1/2-inch disks in detail.

When you purchase floppy disks for your computer, you need to purchase the correct disk size to match your disk drive type. If you don't know your disk drive size, your original computer receipt should specify the disk types. If you can't locate the disk type, Table 7-3 lists probable disk types for various computers.

The FORMAT command prepares (or formats) a disk for use on your computer. If your floppy disk size matches your disk drive size, formatting is easy. However, if you are formatting a disk whose storage capabilities are smaller than those of your disk drive, you must add one or more qualifiers in the FORMAT command line.

Name	Characteristics	Storage Capacity
720KB	Single-sided, double-density	737,280 bytes
1.44MB	Double-sided, double-density	1,457,664 bytes

Table 7-2. Common 3 1/2-Inch Disk Types

Computer	Probable Floppy	Disk Type
Original IBM PC or PC clone	360KB	5 1/4"
Older laptop computer, older PS/2	720KB	3 1/2"
IBM PC, AT, AT compatible, 386 machines	1.2MB	5 1/4"
New PS/2, 386 machines	1.44MB	3 1/2"

Table 7-3. Probable Floppy Disk Sizes for Different Computer Types

The FORMAT command first divides your disk into circular tracks.

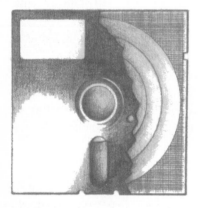

Understanding Formatting

DOS stores information on your disk by magnetically recording the contents of a file on the surface of the disk. Because your disk may eventually store hundreds of files, DOS must remember exactly where it stores the contents of each file. Formatting essentially divides your disk into a fixed number of storage locations that DOS can later use to store files.

Disk Formatting

Disk formatting is the process of preparing your disk for use with a specific computer. The FORMAT command enables DOS to perform the formatting process. During formatting, FORMAT divides your disk into storage regions called tracks and sectors. The number of sectors on your disk depends on the disk's storage capabilities. As FORMAT creates the disk sectors, DOS checks each sector to ensure that the sector can store information. If the sector is damaged and incapable of storing information, FORMAT marks the sector as bad, thus preventing DOS from using the bad sector.

To begin, the FORMAT command tells DOS to divide the disk into several concentric circles called *tracks*. These tracks are similar to the grooves that appear on the surface of a record album.

Next, the FORMAT command tells DOS to further divide each circular track into pie-shaped storage bins called *sectors*. DOS eventually stores information for a file within each sector.

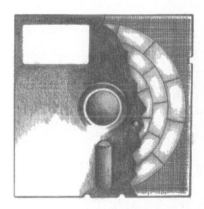

The number of tracks and sectors the FORMAT command creates depends on your disk type. As the FORMAT command divides your tracks into sectors, DOS checks each sector to ensure that the sector is capable of storing information. The disk's surface could have been damaged during manufacturing, making it incapable of storing information in a few places (although improved disk quality is making this less common).

The FORMAT command divides each track into pie-shaped sectors, within which DOS later stores information.

When DOS encounters a damaged sector, FORMAT marks the sector as unusable. This marking prevents DOS from attempting to store information in the damaged sector.

Formatting a Disk Whose Size Matches Your Disk Drive

If you are formatting a floppy disk whose size matches your disk drive size, the formatting process is easy. An example of such a match is a 1.2MB disk in a 1.2MB drive. On the other hand, a 360KB disk has a smaller capacity than that which can be accessed with a 1.2MB drive.

Using the CHDIR command, select the DOS directory as the current directory:

```
C:\> CHDIR \DOS <ENTER>
C:\DOS>
```

Now issue the following DIR command:

```
C:\DOS> DIR FORMAT.COM <ENTER>

 Volume in drive C has no label
 Volume Serial Number is 1A43-5E8B
 Directory of C:\DOS

FORMAT   COM    22717 01-28-93   6:00a
        1 file(s)      22717 bytes
                     9361408 bytes free
```

The FORMAT.COM file contains the FORMAT command. To format an unused disk in drive A, issue the following FORMAT command. When you press ENTER to execute the command, FORMAT will prompt you to insert a disk into drive A:

```
C:\DOS> FORMAT A: <ENTER>
Insert new diskette for drive A:
and press ENTER when ready...
```

If you have inserted an unused disk into drive A and closed its drive latch, press ENTER to continue. If you want to cancel the FORMAT command, press the CTRL-C keyboard combination. This cancels the FORMAT command, returning control to the DOS prompt.

Warning: As a result of the formatting process, the FORMAT command will destroy the current contents of the disk in drive A. Only use FORMAT on an unused disk! Should you accidentally format the wrong disk, DOS versions 5 and 6 provide the UNFORMAT command that you can use to salvage the disk's data.

Next, depending on your DOS version, FORMAT may display additional messages, for example, that it is verifying the disk size or that it is saving unformatted information. Next, FORMAT displays (depending on your version of DOS) either a message on your screen indicating how much of the disk it has formatted or a message stating the side and track (referred to as head and cylinder) it is currently formatting.

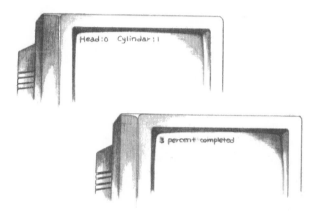

Depending on your version of DOS, the FORMAT command will display a message that tells you either the current head and cylinder (that is, the side of the disk and the track number) or what percentage of the disk has been formatted.

Depending on your DOS version, FORMAT may prompt you to type in a disk volume name.

```
Volume label (11 characters, ENTER for none)?
```

A *volume label* is an optional name you assign to your disk. If you are creating a floppy disk to store letters, you might assign the disk label LETTERS. If you are storing Lotus 1-2-3 spreadsheets, you might name the disk LOTUS or 123.

Next, FORMAT displays summary messages about the disk size and storage units.

```
Format complete
   nnnnnn bytes total disk space
   nnnnnn bytes available on disk
```

If the disk contains damaged sectors, FORMAT displays the amount of disk space that it has marked as unusable.

```
Format complete
   nnnnnn bytes total disk space
     nnnn bytes in bad sectors
   nnnnnn bytes available on disk
```

Depending on your DOS version, FORMAT may display a message stating the disk's serial number. Finally, FORMAT asks you if you want to format additional disks.

```
Format another (Y/N)?
```

If you want to format an additional disk, type **Y** and press ENTER. FORMAT prompts you to insert a disk in drive A, repeating the formatting process. If you type **N** and press ENTER, FORMAT ends and returns control to the DOS prompt.

Formatting a Lower-Capacity Disk

If you are using a 1.2MB disk drive, you may need to provide a disk containing files to another user who only has a 360KB drive. To assist you in doing so, FORMAT lets you format a disk whose storage capacity is smaller than your drive size.

Simply placing the smaller-capacity disk in the drive is not enough—you must tell FORMAT that it is to format a lower-capacity disk. This is done through the use of command line qualifiers immediately after the FORMAT command. Table 7-4 shows some of the qualifiers that can be used with FORMAT. To format a 360KB floppy disk in a 1.2MB drive, you must include the /4 qualifier in FORMAT's command line:

```
C:\DOS> FORMAT A: /4
```

The /4 qualifier tells FORMAT that although you are using a 1.2MB drive, you want to format a 360KB disk. Once FORMAT begins formatting the disk, the processing that appears on your screen is identical to a standard disk size format operation.

Formatting a Bootable System Disk

As discussed in Chapter 3, to start DOS you must use a *system disk*. A system disk differs from other DOS disks in that it contains two special *hidden files*. A hidden file is one that resides on disk but does not appear in

Drive Size	Drive Capacity	Desired Capacity	Qualifier
5 1/4"	1.2MB	360KB	/4
3 1/2"	1.44MB	720KB	/F:720

Table 7-4. The FORMAT /4 and /F Qualifiers

the directory listing. DOS hides these important files to prevent you from renaming or accidentally deleting them. The FORMAT command /S qualifier directs FORMAT to place these hidden files on the newly formatted disk. The only time you need to include the /S qualifier is when you are creating a disk that must start DOS, such as the first time you format your hard disk. In most cases, you won't want to place these hidden system files on your new disks because of the amount of disk space the files consume. If you don't need to start your computer by using the floppy disk, you shouldn't put these system files on the disk.

The following FORMAT command creates a bootable disk using the /S option.

```
C:\DOS> FORMAT A: /S
```

When the command is completed, FORMAT displays a message indicating that the system files have been transferred to the new disk, as well as the amount of space the system files consumed.

```
Format complete
 System transferred
  nnnnnn bytes total disk space
   nnnnn bytes used by system
  nnnnnn bytes available on disk
```

If you are formatting a bootable disk whose storage capability is smaller than your disk drive, simply combine /S with /4 or /F, as shown here.

```
C:\DOS> FORMAT A: /4 /S
```

Creating a Bootable Disk

A bootable or system disk is a disk containing two hidden files required by DOS. A hidden file is a file that is stored in a directory but does not appear in a directory listing.

The FORMAT command lets you create a bootable file by copying the two hidden system files to a newly formatted disk. To create a bootable disk, you must include the /S qualifier in your FORMAT command line, as shown here:

C:\DOS> FORMAT A:/S

Because these two hidden files consume a considerable amount of disk space, you shouldn't need to place these files on your disk.

Keys to Success

To prepare a disk to store information, you must use the FORMAT command. The FORMAT command first divides your disk into circular regions called tracks, similar to the grooves on a record album. Next, FORMAT further divides each track into pie-shaped storage bins called sectors. DOS uses the tracks and sectors to store and locate information on the disk.

When you format a floppy disk, you must be aware of the floppy disk's capacity, as well as the capacity of your disk drive. If you are formatting a disk whose storage capacity is the same as that of your disk drive, the format process is straightforward. If your disk capacity is smaller than that of the disk drive, you must include either the /4 or /F qualifier to inform FORMAT of the smaller disk size.

If you need to create a bootable system disk, you must invoke FORMAT with the /S qualifier. When you include /S, FORMAT will transfer the hidden system files to your newly formatted disk. Because most disks aren't used to boot DOS, placing these system files on the disk unnecessarily consumes disk space.

Note: Should you accidentally format the wrong disk, DOS 5 and 6 provide an UNFORMAT command.

What Do They Mean by...?

Double-Density and Quad-Density Disks Density refers to the amount of information your disk can store in an area of a fixed size. When disk manufacturers improved the capabilities of disks and disk drives so that a disk could store twice as much information as the original 180K disks, they named these disks *double-density disks.* When technology improvements allowed even more information to be squeezed on the disk, the new disks were termed *quad-density* (meaning that the disk could essentially store four times as much information).

Disk Cylinders The FORMAT command divides a disk into circular tracks similar to the grooves on a record album. For hard disks, these tracks are often referred to as *cylinders.* For your purposes, you can use the terms tracks and cylinders interchangeably.

Learning the Essential File Manipulation Commands

Chapter 5 discussed how DOS stores information in files on your disk. Chapter 6 discussed ways to organize your files by grouping related files into directories. The files you store in directories may be letters, reports, spreadsheets, or even programs. Every file in your directory must have a unique name. You use the DIR command to display file names and extensions, file sizes, and other file-related information.

If you work with paper files in an office, you know that at times you must do more than look in the file cabinet to see what is there. Sometimes you need to copy a file's contents, change the name assigned to a file, look through a file's contents, or throw away an unnecessary file. These four filing tasks (copying, renaming, viewing, and discarding) also apply to files stored on your disk. To perform these operations on your computer, you use the COPY, RENAME, TYPE, and DEL commands. Regardless of how you use your computer, you must understand files and these four simple file manipulation commands. This chapter helps you master these essential commands.

File Operations

Working with paper files or with files stored on your disk involves four common operations: copying, renaming, viewing, and discarding. To perform these operations, DOS provides four file manipulation commands.

COPY	Copies one file's contents to another file
RENAME	Renames an existing file
TYPE	Displays a file's contents on your screen
DEL	Deletes a file from your disk

Copying a File's Contents to Another File

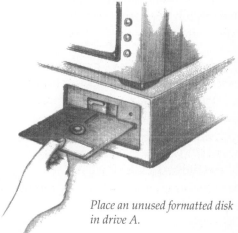

The COPY command enables you to copy one file's contents to another file, or to another disk. For hard disk users, COPY is used most often to copy a file they have created with a word processor or spreadsheet program to a floppy disk for later use by someone else.

Place an unused formatted disk in drive A.

To see how COPY works, place a newly formatted disk in your floppy drive A.

Next, use the CHDIR command to select the DOS directory as the current directory:

```
C:\> CHDIR \DOS  <ENTER>
C:\DOS>
```

In this case, you will be copying the file LABEL.EXE from the DOS directory to the floppy disk in drive A. To perform the copy operation, issue the following command:

```
C:\DOS> COPY LABEL.EXE A: <ENTER>
```

When you press ENTER, the activation light on your hard disk illuminates briefly as DOS reads the file LABEL.EXE from your hard disk. Then the floppy disk's activation light illuminates as DOS writes the file to the floppy disk. When the copy operation completes, COPY displays the following information:

```
C:\DOS> COPY LABEL.EXE A: <ENTER>
     1 file(s) copied
C:\DOS>
```

The file LABEL.EXE was used in this example because it is a file every DOS user has on disk. The file could just as easily have been a file from your word processor or spreadsheet program.

To use the COPY command, you must know two things: the name of the file you want to copy and the location (or name) of the file to which you want the file copied. The file you are copying is often called the *source file*.

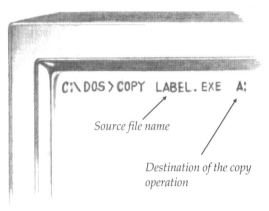

Source file name

Destination of the copy operation

Every copy operation for files has a source file whose contents are copied and a destination to which the files are copied. This command copies the file LABEL.EXE to the floppy disk in drive A.

The location to which you are copying the file is called the *destination*. For example, the previous command used LABEL.EXE as the file to copy (the source) and drive A as the destination.

If you perform a directory listing of drive A, you can verify that the copy operation was indeed successful.

```
C:\DOS> DIR A:   <ENTER>


 Volume in drive A has no label
 Volume Serial Number is 0E2F-08E1
 Directory of A:\

LABEL     EXE      9390 01-28-93    6:00a
      1 file(s)          9390 bytes
                       352256 bytes free
```

The COPY command created an exact duplicate of LABEL.EXE on drive A. In some cases, however, you may want to assign a different name to the destination file. The following COPY command copies the file LABEL.EXE to drive A and assigns to the destination copy the name MYLABEL.EXE.

```
C:\DOS> COPY LABEL.EXE A:MYLABEL.EXE <ENTER>
      1 file(s) copied
```

In this case, the destination contains the desired drive letter (A:) as well as the desired file name. A directory listing of drive A reveals the new file:

```
C:\DOS> DIR A:   <ENTER>


 Volume in drive A has no label
 Volume Serial Number is 0E2F-08E1
 Directory of A:\

LABEL     EXE      9390 01-28-93    6:00a
MYLABEL   EXE      9390 01-28-93    6:00a
      2 file(s)         18780 bytes
                       342016 bytes free
```

Warning: If you specify the name of an existing file as the destination of a file copy operation, COPY overwrites the existing file and the file's contents will be lost!

The following COPY command copies the file FORMAT.COM to the disk in drive A and assigns the new file the name MYLABEL.EXE:

```
C:\DOS> COPY FORMAT.COM A:MYLABEL.EXE <ENTER>
    1 file(s) copied
```

COPY does not care that you already had a file on drive A named MYLABEL.EXE. Instead, COPY overwrites the contents of the previous file. To prevent COPY from overwriting a file, use DIR to determine if a file exists with the same name as the destination file before you perform the file copy operation. For example, if you want to copy the file FORMAT.COM to drive A, you can test if drive A already has a file by the same name.

```
C:\DOS> DIR A:FORMAT.COM <ENTER>
File not found
```

The "File not found" message tells you that you can copy FORMAT.COM to drive A without overwriting an existing file.

Copying Files from Your Floppy Disk to Your Hard Disk

Just as you might need to copy files onto a floppy disk to give to another user, you might also need to copy files from a floppy disk to your hard disk. Use the CHDIR command to change to the directory into which you want to copy the files. Then issue the COPY command to copy the files from the floppy disk. Be sure to specify in the source file name the drive letter for the floppy disk.

To better understand this process, use MKDIR to create the directory \TESTCOPY, then use CHDIR to change to the newly created directory:

```
C:\DOS> MKDIR \TESTCOPY <ENTER>
C:\DOS> CHDIR \TESTCOPY <ENTER>
C:\TESTCOPY>
```

With the disk containing the file MYLABEL.EXE in drive A, issue the following COPY command:

```
C:\TESTCOPY> COPY A:MYLABEL.EXE MYLABEL.EXE <ENTER>
```

When you press ENTER, you first see the activation light for your floppy disk illuminate as COPY reads the file. Next, you will see the activation light on the hard disk come on as COPY writes the file.

As before, the COPY command contains a source and destination file name. You have copied MYLABEL.EXE from drive A to the current directory (\TESTCOPY) on your hard disk.

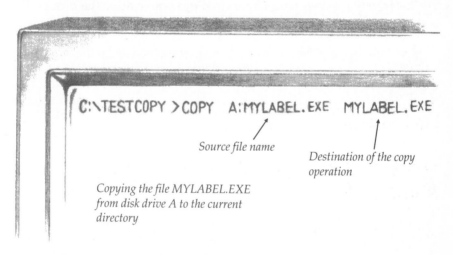

C:\TESTCOPY >COPY A:MYLABEL.EXE MYLABEL.EXE

Source file name

Destination of the copy operation

Copying the file MYLABEL.EXE from disk drive A to the current directory

Understanding COPY's Most Common Errors

Copying a file to or from a different disk is quite straightforward. You simply type COPY followed by the name of the file you want to copy and then the location to which you want the file copied. As with all DOS commands, however, there is the possibility for error. This section describes COPY's most common errors and how to correct them.

If COPY cannot locate the source file you want to copy, it displays the following message:

```
C:\> COPY XXX A: <ENTER>
File not found - XXX
    0 file(s) copied
```

If this message appears, check the following:

- Is the source file name spelled correctly?
- Does the source file reside in the current directory? Use DIR to find out. If the file does not reside in the current directory, use CHDIR to select the correct directory.
- If the file resides on another disk, did you include the proper disk drive letter?

If you are copying the file from one disk to another, and if the destination disk does not have room for the file, COPY displays this message:

```
C:\> COPY BIGFILE.TXT A: <ENTER>
Insufficient disk space
    0 file(s) copied
```

If this error message occurs, you must copy the file to a new disk, or you must make more room on the destination disk by deleting unnecessary files.

When you perform a file copy operation, you must specify a destination drive, directory, or a file name that is different from the source file. If you try to copy a file to its same directory, without changing the name of the file, COPY displays the following:

```
C:\DOS> COPY FORMAT.COM FORMAT.COM <ENTER>
File cannot be copied onto itself
    0 file(s) copied
```

Remember, every file name in a directory must be unique. You cannot have two copies of the same file in the same directory with the same name. This error message is most common when you are trying to copy a file to or from another disk and you forget to specify a disk drive letter in front of one of the files.

The COPY Command

The COPY command lets you copy a file from one disk or directory to another. To use COPY, you must specify the name of the file you want to copy and the location to which you want the file copied. The following command copies the file BUDGET.LTR from the current directory to the disk in drive A:

C:\WP> COPY BUDGET.LTR A: <ENTER>

Renaming an Existing File

Remember, every file on your disk should have a meaningful name that describes the file's contents. As you work with your computer, you may encounter poorly named files or files whose names no longer accurately describe the file's contents. Just as you might assign a new name to a paper file, the RENAME command lets you rename a file on your disk.

The following RENAME command changes the name of the file MYLABEL.EXE to NEWLABEL.EXE:

```
C:\TESTCOPY> RENAME MYLABEL.EXE NEWLABEL.EXE <ENTER>
```

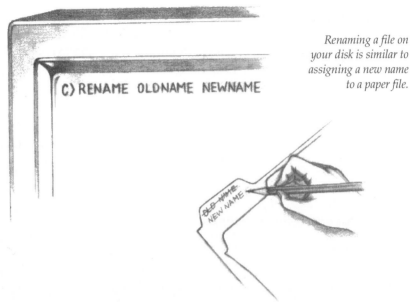

Renaming a file on your disk is similar to assigning a new name to a paper file.

A directory listing reveals the new file name:

```
C:\TESTCOPY> DIR   <ENTER>


 Volume in drive C has no label
 Volume Serial Number is 1A43-5E8B
 Directory of C:\TESTCOPY

 .            <DIR>      02-15-93   1:29p
 ..           <DIR>      02-15-93   1:29p
 MYLABEL   EXE    22717 01-28-93   6:00a
         3 file(s)      22717 bytes
                      9318400 bytes free
```

Because of its frequency of use, DOS lets you abbreviate the RENAME command as simply REN. Using REN, the following command changes the file NEWLABEL.EXE to DELETEME.EXE:

```
C:\TESTCOPY> REN NEWLABEL.EXE DELETEME.EXE <ENTER>
```

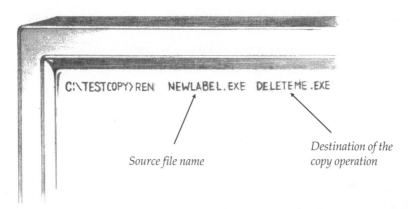

C:\TESTCOPY> REN NEWLABEL.EXE DELETEME.EXE

Source file name

Destination of the copy operation

To rename a file on your disk, specify the old name of the file, followed by the new name.

Like the COPY command, RENAME requires a source and destination file name. In this case, the source name is the name of the file you want to rename, and the destination name is the new name you want to assign to the file.

Understanding RENAME's Most Common Errors

The best way to avoid errors with RENAME is to use RENAME only with files that reside in the current directory.

The RENAME command assigns a new name to an existing file. It does not (and cannot) move the file from one disk or directory to another. If you attempt to move a file by using RENAME, the command fails. For example, the following command attempts to move the file DELETEME.EXE from the directory TESTCOPY on drive C to the current directory of drive A:

```
C:\> RENAME DELETEME.EXE A:DELETEME.EXE <ENTER>
Invalid parameter
```

RENAME displays the "Invalid parameter" message to tell you that either the source name or the destination name is invalid. In this case, the drive letter (A:) before the destination name is invalid because it directs

RENAME to move the file from the current directory (instead of simply renaming the file).

RENAME does not change a file name to a name that already exists in the directory. If you attempt to do so, RENAME displays an error message stating that a duplicate file with the specified name already exists. Thus, the command fails.

Using drive A as the current drive, the following command attempts to rename the file LABEL.EXE as MYLABEL.EXE. Because the file MYLABEL.EXE already exists, the command fails.

```
A:\> REN LABEL.EXE MYLABEL.EXE <ENTER>
Duplicate file name or file not found
```

If RENAME cannot locate the file you want to rename, it will display this same message. In this case, use the DIR command to be sure that you are spelling the name correctly and that the file resides in the current directory.

The RENAME Command

The RENAME command lets you change the name of an existing disk file. Because of its frequency of use, DOS lets you abbreviate RENAME as simply REN. The following RENAME command renames the file OLDNAME.LTR to NEWNAME.LTR:

C:\WP> REN OLDNAME.LTR NEWNAME.LTR <ENTER>

Deleting Files from Your Disk

There are many times in an office when you no longer need the information stored in a paper file; the same is true for files on your disk. The DEL command deletes files from your disk when the files are no longer needed.

C) DEL OLDFILE

Deleting a file from your disk is similar to throwing away a paper file.

Warning: If you inadvertently delete the wrong file, you may not be able to retrieve the contents of the file. Disk utility programs are available to help you recover from errant commands that damage files on your disk. If you have one of these utility programs, you may be able to "undelete" a file.

Because an errant DEL command can have catastrophic effects, you must use DEL with caution. If you are careful, you shouldn't experience any problems.

To delete a file, you simply place the file's name immediately after the DEL command. For example, the following command deletes the file MYLABEL.EXE from the disk in drive A:

```
C:\TESTCOPY> DEL A:MYLABEL.EXE <ENTER>
```

When you press ENTER, the activation light for drive A illuminates briefly as DEL removes the file. A directory listing of drive A shows DEL has successfully deleted the file.

```
C:\TESTCOPY> DIR A:   <ENTER>

Volume in drive A has no label
Volume Serial Number is 0E2F-08E1
Directory of A:\

LABEL    EXE     9390 01-28-93   6:00a
         1 file(s)       9390 bytes
                       352256 bytes free
```

The following DEL command deletes the file DELETEME.EXE from the current directory.

```
C:\TESTCOPY> DEL DELETEME.EXE <ENTER>
```

The DEL command only deletes files from your disk. DEL does not remove directories. To remove the TESTCOPY directory, you must first use CHDIR to select a different directory from the current directory and then use RMDIR to remove the directory. (For details on changing and removing directories, review Chapter 6.)

Understanding DEL's Most Common Errors

To use the DEL command, specify the name of the file you want to delete and press ENTER. The most common error with the DEL command occurs when DEL cannot locate the file to delete.

```
C:\> DEL FILENAME.EXT
File not found
```

If DEL displays the "File not found" error message, be sure that you are spelling the file name correctly and the t the file resides in the current directory.

As you begin working with advanced DOS commands, you will learn that it is possible to protect your files from being inadvertently deleted by assigning them the *read-only* attribute, which prevents files from being changed or removed. If you attempt to delete a read-only file, DEL displays the following message:

```
C:\> DEL FILENAME.EXT <ENTER>
Access denied
```

For more information on read-only files, refer to the ATTRIB command in your DOS manual or see the book *DOS Inside & Out*, available from Osborne/McGraw-Hill.

The DEL Command

The DEL command lets you delete a file from your disk when the file is no longer needed. The following command deletes the file REPORT.OLD.

C:\> DEL REPORT.OLD <ENTER>

Warning: *If you inadvertently delete the wrong file, you must use a special disk utility program to retrieve the file's contents.*

Moving a File from One Directory to Another

If you are using DOS 6, the MOVE command lets you move a file from one directory to another. Prior to DOS 6, if you wanted to move a file, you had to first copy the file to the new directory and then delete the original from the old directory. The MOVE command, however, lets you move the file in one step. The following command, for example, would move the file FILENAME.EXT from the current directory, SUBDIR, to the directory NEWDIR:

```
C:\SUBDIR> MOVE FILENAME.EXT \NEWDIR\FILENAME.EXT   <ENTER>
```

The MOVE command fully supports the DOS wildcard characters. As such, the following command would move all of the files having the BAT extension in the current directory to the BATCH directory:

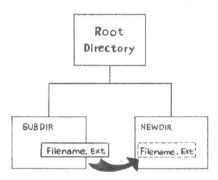

The DOS 6 MOVE command lets you move a file from one directory to another.

```
C:\SUBDIR> MOVE *.BAT \BATCH\*.*   <ENTER>
```

The MOVE command will also let you move a file from one disk to another. The following command, for example, moves the file FILENAME.EXT from the current directory to the root directory on drive A:

```
C:\SUBDIR> MOVE FILENAME.EXT A:\FILENAME.EXT   <ENTER>
```

If the directory to which you are moving a file contains another file with the same name as the file you are moving, MOVE will over write the existing file's contents.

Viewing the Contents of a File

As discussed in previous chapters, files are used for storing programs, spreadsheets, word processing documents, and other information. A text file is a file that contains the letters and numbers you would expect to see on a page of text.

The TYPE command lets you view on your screen the contents of a file. Many software programs provide a file named READ.ME on the installation disk. The file typically contains additional instructions about how to use the program. To display the file's contents on your screen, you would use TYPE as follows:

```
C:\> TYPE A:READ.ME <ENTER>
```

Text files are different from word processor files. As you know, a word processor lets you create reports and letters by aligning margins, centering text, and letting you **bold** or *italicize* key words. To accomplish these tasks, word processors embed special characters within your documents that provide unique instructions for the word processor. If you use the TYPE command to display the contents of a document, your screen will display some recognizable text intermixed with the meaningless characters that provide directions to your word processor. If this occurs, you must use the word processor that created the file to properly view the contents of the document.

Files that contain programs or DOS commands are called *binary files*. The TYPE command cannot display in a meaningful manner the contents of a binary file. If you try to view the contents of an EXE or COM file (which are binary files), your screen will fill with meaningless characters.

Understanding TYPE's Most Common Errors

If TYPE cannot locate the file you specify in the command line, it displays the following message:

```
C:\> TYPE FILENAME.EXT <ENTER>
File not found - FILENAME.EXT
```

Should this error occur, be sure that you are spelling the file name correctly, and that the file resides in the current directory.

Another common error when using the TYPE command is trying to display the contents of a non-text file. When you use TYPE to display such a file, your screen fills with meaningless characters.

The TYPE Command

The TYPE command displays the contents of a text file. A text file is a file that contains only standard letters and numbers. The following TYPE command displays the contents of a file named AUTOEXEC.BAT that commonly resides in the root directory.

C:\> TYPE \AUTOEXEC.BAT <ENTER>

Keys to Success

Whether you are working with paper files in an office or with files stored on disk, the operations you commonly perform are the same: copying, renaming, deleting, and viewing. To perform these operations, DOS provides four essential file manipulation commands: COPY, RENAME, DEL, and TYPE.

The COPY command copies a file's contents from one disk or directory to another. To use the COPY command, you must know the name of the file you want to copy as well as the location to which you want to copy the file.

The RENAME command lets you change the name of an existing file on your disk. Because of its frequency of use, DOS lets you abbreviate RE-NAME as simply REN. To use RENAME, you must know the name of the file you want to rename, and the new name of the file.

The DEL command deletes a file from your disk. To use DEL, you must know the name of the file you want to delete.

If you are using DOS 6, the MOVE command lets you move a file from one directory to another, or from one disk to another.

The TYPE command lets you view on your screen the contents of a text file. A text file is a file that contains only letters and numbers. To use TYPE, you must know the name of the text file whose contents you want to display.

What Do They Mean by...?

ASCII File   An ASCII file is another name for a text file. ASCII files contain only the letters and numbers you would expect to see on a typed page. Most word processors provide a way of creating ASCII files. The TYPE command lets you view an ASCII file's contents.

Read-Only File   A read-only file is a file whose contents DOS can read, but cannot change or delete. The ATTRIB command lets you set a file to read-only.

Accessing Files Stored in Different Directories

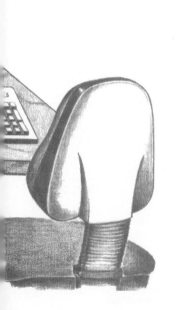

You used the MKDIR command in Chapter 6 for creating different directories to help organize your files. Once the additional directories exist on your disk, you use the CHDIR command to change from one directory to another. Using CHDIR to select a directory is similar to opening a drawer of a filing cabinet to access specific files.

Depending on your directory structure and different software applications, you may find yourself repeatedly changing from one directory to another to perform daily tasks. Although you know how to use CHDIR to change directories, changing from one directory to another may become quite time-consuming. This chapter discusses how to quickly and directly access files that reside in a different directory.

Using DOS Path Names

Remember that when you work with directories, you must specify a complete path name to the directory. Path names provide DOS with a road map to a directory or file. In many cases, your directory path name begins at the root directory and may continue several levels.

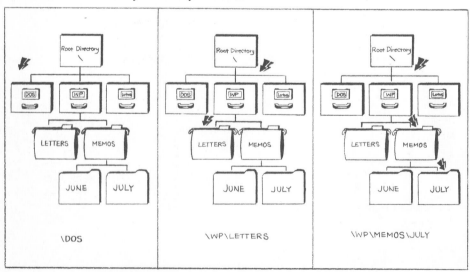

Depending on your directory structure, your path names may contain several levels of directory names.

If you know the directory name where a file resides on disk, you can access the file by preceding the file name with the complete path name of the file's directory. For example, the FORMAT command resides in the DOS directory. By preceding the file name for the FORMAT command with a complete path name, the following DIR command displays a directory listing for FORMAT.COM, regardless of the current directory:

```
C:\> DIR \DOS\FORMAT.COM <ENTER>


Volume in drive C has no label
Volume Serial Number is 1A43-5E8B
Directory of C:\DOS

FORMAT   COM     22717 01-28-93    6:00a
         1 file(s)      22717 bytes
                      9361408 bytes free
```

To locate the file FORMAT.COM in this example, DIR begins at the root directory and searches the directory DOS.

To copy, rename, or delete a file that resides in a different directory, you must precede the file name with a complete directory path. To better understand this process, use the MKDIR command to create a directory named TESTDIR, and then use CHDIR to change to the new directory.

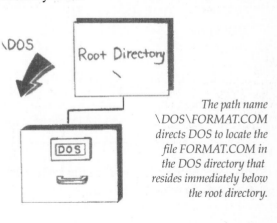

The path name \DOS\FORMAT.COM directs DOS to locate the file FORMAT.COM in the DOS directory that resides immediately below the root directory.

```
C:\> MKDIR \TESTDIR <ENTER>
C:\> CHDIR \TESTDIR <ENTER>
C:\TESTDIR>
```

Using a complete path name to the file FORMAT.COM, copy the file from the DOS directory to the current directory, as shown here:

```
C:\TESTDIR> COPY \DOS\FORMAT.COM FORMAT.COM <ENTER>
     1 file(s) copied
```

A directory listing of the current directory reveals that the copy operation was successful.

```
C:\TESTDIR> DIR   <ENTER>

  Volume in drive C has no label
  Volume Serial Number is 1A43-5E8B
  Directory of C:\TESTDIR

  .               <DIR>       02-15-93    1:29p
  ..              <DIR>       02-15-93    1:29p
  FORMAT    COM       22717  01-28-93    6:00a
          3 file(s)          22717 bytes
                           9328640 bytes free
```

Repeat this process to copy the file LABEL.EXE from the DOS directory to the current directory TESTDIR.

```
C:\TESTDIR> COPY \DOS\LABEL.EXE LABEL.EXE <ENTER>
     1 file(s) copied
```

As before, a directory listing of TESTDIR shows that the file copy operation was successful.

```
C:\> DIR  <ENTER>

  Volume in drive C has no label
  Volume Serial Number is 1A43-5E8B
  Directory of C:\TESTDIR

  .              <DIR>      02-15-93   1:29p
  ..             <DIR>      02-15-93   1:29p
  FORMAT   COM     22717 01-28-93   6:00a
  LABEL    EXE      9390 01-28-93   6:00a
        4 file(s)       32107 bytes
                      9316352 bytes free
```

Use the CHDIR command to select the root directory as the current directory.

```
C:\TESTDIR> CHDIR \ <ENTER>
C:\>
```

Next, specify the complete path name to the file LABEL.EXE in the TESTDIR directory and use the DEL command to delete the file:

```
C:\>  DEL \TESTDIR\LABEL.EXE <ENTER>
```

You can verify that the file was deleted by using the DIR command.

```
C:\TESTDIR> DIR  <ENTER>

Volume in drive C has no label
Volume Serial Number is 1A43-5E8B
Directory of C:\TESTDIR

.            <DIR>      02-15-93   1:29p
..           <DIR>      02-15-93   1:29p
FORMAT   COM    22717 01-28-93   6:00a
      3 file(s)        22717 bytes
                     9328640 bytes free
```

Complete Path Names

Unless told to do otherwise, DOS always looks for files in the current directory. If you want to access a file in a different directory, you must tell DOS the name of the directory containing the file. You must specify a complete path name in order to do this.

For example, the following command tells DOS to copy the file DISKCOPY.COM from the DOS directory to the disk in drive A.

C:\> COPY \DOS\DISKCOPY.COM A: <ENTER>

The complete path name \DOS\DISKCOPY.COM tells DOS to locate the file DISKCOPY.COM in the DOS directory, which resides immediately below the root directory.

Executing Commands That Reside in a Different Directory

Remember that DOS has two types of commands: internal and external. Internal commands include commands such as CLS, MKDIR, and CHDIR. Because of their frequency of use, DOS always stores internal commands in memory so they can be executed quickly. External commands, on the other hand, are stored in disk files and are given the EXE or COM extensions. When you execute an external command, DOS must locate the command's file on disk, load the file into memory, and then execute the command.

Unless you tell DOS to look elsewhere, DOS only looks for files in the current directory. In Chapter 7, for example, you used the FORMAT command to prepare floppy disks for use by DOS. Before you ran the FORMAT command, you used the CHDIR command to select the DOS directory as the current directory. As a result, when you entered the external command name (FORMAT), DOS was able to locate the file FORMAT.COM in the DOS directory.

If you had to continually change directories every time you wanted to execute an external command, you could waste considerable time. However, DOS provides an easier way to execute such commands.

If you want to execute an external command that does not reside in the current directory, you simply precede the command name with the correct directory name. For example, the following command uses a complete path name to the file FORMAT.COM to invoke FORMAT from the TESTDIR directory.

```
C:\TESTDIR> \DOS\FORMAT A: <ENTER>
```

In this case, the complete path name tells DOS to locate the external command FORMAT.COM in the directory that resides immediately below the root.

Simplifying Your Command Execution

Although typing in a complete path name enables you to invoke a command that resides in a different directory, it increases the amount of typing you must perform, and therefore the possibility of making mistakes. To make it easier (and faster) for you to execute your commonly used external commands, DOS allows you to define a list of directories that it automatically searches each time you type in an external command.

Executing External Commands in Another Directory

External commands are programs with EXE or COM extensions that are stored on disk. When you execute an external command, DOS must first locate the command on disk and then load it into your computer's memory. By default, when you type in an external command name, DOS searches the current directory for the command. If the external command resides in a directory other than the current directory, you must tell DOS how to locate the command. To do so, simply precede the command name with the directory path to the program file.

For example, the following command from the current directory TESTDIR invokes the LABEL command that resides in the DOS directory.

    C:\TESTDIR> \DOS\LABEL A: <ENTER>

By using the path name as its road map, DOS finds the command file LABEL.EXE in the directory DOS, which resides immediately below the root.

For example, the DOS directory contains many commonly used commands. If you tell DOS always to search that directory for external commands, you can invoke all the DOS commands without having to type a complete path name for each command.

The PATH command lets you define the list of directories to be searched by DOS for external commands. If another user has installed DOS on your system for you, you may already have a command path defined. To view your system's current command path, type PATH at the DOS prompt and press ENTER.

```
C:\> PATH <ENTER>
```

If a command path exists, this command displays the names of every directory that DOS automatically searches for external commands. If a command path is not defined, DOS displays the message "No path."

A command path is a list of directory names separated by semicolons. For example, the following PATH command directs DOS to automatically search the DOS directory, as well as the root, for external commands:

```
C:\> PATH C:\DOS;C:\ <ENTER>
```

Once you define a command path and then execute an external command, DOS first determines whether the specified command resides in the current directory. If DOS finds the command, it is executed. If DOS fails to locate the command in the current directory, DOS checks to see if you have defined a command path. If you have, DOS begins searching (in the specified order) each directory in the path for the file. If DOS locates the external command in one of the directories, it executes the command. If none of the directories in the path contain the command, DOS displays the following message:

```
Bad command or file name
```

Using the following command path,

C:\DOS;C:\

DOS first searches for the command in the current directory, followed by the directory C:\DOS, and lastly the root directory on drive C. If you have several directories that contain commonly used commands, consider placing the name of each directory in the command path.

Chapter 10 discusses a special file named AUTOEXEC.BAT in which you can place one or more commands you want DOS to automatically execute each time your system starts. Most users will place a PATH command in AUTOEXEC.BAT so DOS automatically knows which directories to search for external commands each time the system starts.

The PATH Command

By default, when you enter an external command, DOS only searches for the command in the current directory. If you want to execute an external command that does not reside in the current directory, you must precede the command name with a complete path name.

The PATH command enables you to specify one or more directories that you want DOS to automatically search each time you issue an external command. By defining a command path that includes the directories likely to contain your commonly used commands, you can simplify execution. Once you specify a command's directory in the command path, you can invoke the command from any directory simply by typing the command's name at the DOS prompt. The following PATH command, for example, directs DOS to automatically search the DOS directory.

C:\> PATH C:\DOS <ENTER>

In this case, each time DOS fails to locate an external command in the current directory, it automatically searches the DOS directory for the file. If you want DOS to search several directories (such as the DOS directory and the root), separate the directory names in the PATH command with a semicolon:

C:\> PATH C:\DOS;C:\ <ENTER>

Keys to Success

DOS directories exist to improve your file organization. As you work with your computer, you should create directories to group related files. To access a file within a directory, you can use CHDIR to select the directory, and then access the file. Or you can specify a complete path name to the file immediately before the file name. By using the path name technique, you can quickly access a file from any directory, without continually having to change from one directory to another.

Executing a command that resides in another directory is similar to accessing a file stored in another directory. You can use the CHDIR command to select the directory that contains the command, and then execute the command. Or you can precede the command name with a complete path name to invoke the command from any directory.

To simplify the execution of your commonly used commands, the PATH command allows you to specify the names of one or more directories that you want DOS to automatically search each time you enter an external command. When DOS fails to locate an external command in the current directory, it searches (in the specified order) the directories in the command path. If DOS locates the command in one of the directories, it executes the command. If DOS fails to locate the command, it displays an error message.

What Do They Mean by...?

Command Path   The command path is the list of directories DOS automatically searches for your external commands each time it fails to locate a command in the current directory. The PATH command allows you to define the command path. By placing the names of the directories containing your commonly used commands in the command path, you make it much easier to execute external commands.

Complete Path Name   A complete path name is the list of directories, beginning at the root, that DOS must traverse to locate a file. Generally, a complete path name is the road map DOS follows to locate a file. For example, the path name \DOS\FORMAT illustrates a complete path name to the file FORMAT.COM. If a command resides on another disk, include the disk drive letter and a colon in front of the path name.

Using DOS Batch Files to Save Time and Keystrokes

```
C:\> CD DOS
C:\DOS> FORMAT
```

```
C:\> CD  DBASE
C:\DBASE> DB
```

To run a program (or execute a DOS command), you simply type the program's name at the DOS prompt and press ENTER. DOS loads the program into your computer's memory and runs it. When the program completes, DOS redisplays its prompt and waits for you to enter another command.

As you use your computer on a daily basis, you'll begin to execute many related commands in succession. For example, to perform word processing, you probably first select the directory that contains your word processing files as the current directory and then invoke your word processor. If you are using the WordPerfect word processor, you might issue the following commands:

```
C:\> CHDIR \WP51
C:\WP51>
```

To use the Lotus 1-2-3 spreadsheet package, you might issue the following commands:

```
C:\> CHDIR  \123
C:\123> 123
```

To use the application program in both of these examples, you had to issue two commands. In cases where you must type two or more commands in succession, DOS lets you place the command names in a file that has the BAT extension. BAT is an abbreviation for *batch*. A batch file is a file that contains the names of two or more DOS commands. In the previous examples, your batch file names might be RUNWP.BAT and RUN123.BAT.

To use a batch file, simply type the batch file name at the DOS prompt, just like any DOS command. When DOS encounters a batch file, it automatically runs each of the commands in the file, in the order in which they appear. Because DOS takes care of running each command, you simply type the batch file name. This is much easier than having to remember each command name as well as the correct order of execution.

Obviously, batch files reduce your typing and make it much simpler for you to execute related commands. For example, to use WordPerfect you can simply type RUNWP at the DOS prompt to invoke the batch file RUNWP.BAT. When you do so, DOS automatically executes the CHDIR and WP commands for you.

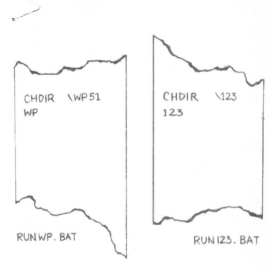

CHDIR   \WP51
WP

RUNWP.BAT

CHDIR   \123
123

RUN123.BAT

Looking at a Few Simple Examples

A batch file is a file containing the names of one or more DOS commands. Batch files have the BAT extension.

A batch file is nothing more than a file that contains the names of DOS commands. You can create a batch file by using your word processor or the DOS editor, or by creating short batch files directly from the keyboard, as discussed in the next section. Consider a simple batch file named TIMEDATE.BAT that uses the CLS command to clear the screen, TIME to set the current system time, and DATE to set the system date.

```
CLS
TIME
DATE
```

To create this batch file, use your word processor to create a file named TIMEDATE.BAT, and then type the three commands in the order shown. Next, save the file in an ASCII format. Some word processors may refer to this as a *text, text-only,* or *non-document* file. After you have created the batch file, simply type TIMEDATE at the DOS prompt and press ENT

```
C:\> TIMEDATE <ENTER>
```

DOS executes, in order, each of the commands in the TIMEDATE.BAT batch file. The CLS command clears your screen display and then TIME displays the familiar prompt for the system time:

```
C:\> TIME
Current time is 10:22:28.40a
ENTER new time:
```

Enter the correct system time, or press ENTER to accept the default time. When the TIME command completes, DOS automatically invokes the DATE command:

```
C:\> DATE
Current date is Mon 04-05-1993
ENTER new date (mm-dd-yy):
```

Either enter the correct system date or press ENTER to leave the current date unchanged. Because DATE is the last command in the batch file, DOS returns control to the DOS prompt after execution of the DATE command. In this example, by typing the batch file name TIMEDATE at the DOS prompt, you directed DOS to perform three related commands.

A batch file can contain one command or as many commands as the available space on your disk will allow. In either case, when you run the batch file, DOS executes the commands contained within the file, in order, one at a time.

Chapter 5 discussed how certain qualifiers enhance the DIR command. The /P qualifier directs DIR to pause with each screenful of files, and the /W qualifier directs DIR to display a wide directory listing containing only file names and extensions. Although these two qualifiers are quite convenient, most users forget they exist.

You can create batch files that include /W and /P so you don't have to remember the exact qualifiers. The batch file WIDEDIR.BAT invokes the DIR command with the /W qualifier. This batch file only contains one command.

```
DIR /W
```

To display the wide directory listing, run WIDEDIR.BAT from the DOS prompt, as shown here:

```
C:\> WIDEDIR <ENTER>
```

The batch file SLOWDIR.BAT uses the /P qualifier to direct DIR to display a direct listing one screen at a time.

```
DIR /P
```

Although these two batch files are quite short, they illustrate how batch files simplify commands that previously may have been difficult to remember.

Batch Files

A batch file is a file that contains the names of one or more DOS commands. Batch files use the BAT extension. When you type a batch file name at the DOS prompt, DOS locates the batch file and executes, in order, all the commands contained in the file.

Batch files simplify the execution of several related commands by allowing you to invoke all the commands in one step. Batch files reduce the amount of typing you must perform, as well as the number of difficult commands you must remember.

Creating Simple Batch Files Directly from Your Keyboard

While it is possible to create batch files by using your word processor, simple batch files can easily be created directly from the keyboard.

Recall that the COPY command enables you to copy one file to another. To copy a file from your keyboard, simply use the device name CON as the source of the file copy operation. CON is the name DOS uses for the keyboard. When you use it as the source for the COPY command, you inform DOS that whatever you type at the keyboard should be copied into the target file. For example, to create a batch file named SHOWVER.BAT that contains the commands CLS and VER, begin by typing the following:

```
C:\> COPY CON SHOWVER.BAT <ENTER>
```

When you press ENTER, DOS moves the cursor to the start of the next line and waits for you to enter the first line of the file. In this case, type **CLS** and press ENTER.

```
C:\> COPY CON SHOWVER.BAT <ENTER>
CLS <ENTER>
```

DOS again advances the cursor and waits for the next line of the file. Type **VER** and press ENTER.

```
C:\> COPY CON SHOWVER.BAT <ENTER>
CLS <ENTER>
VER <ENTER>
```

DOS is now waiting for the next line of the file. Press the F6 function key to tell DOS that no more lines remain to be typed. DOS displays **^Z** (pronounced *Control-Z*). This *end-of-file character* signifies that you have finished entering lines.

```
C:\> COPY CON SHOWVER.BAT <ENTER>
CLS <ENTER>
VER <ENTER>
^Z
```

When you press ENTER, DOS creates the file SHOWVER.BAT and displays the following message:

```
C:\> COPY CON SHOWVER.BAT <ENTER>
CLS <ENTER>
VER <ENTER>
^Z <ENTER>
     1 file(s) copied

C:\>
```

By using the TYPE command, you can view the contents of this batch file.

```
C:\> TYPE SHOWVER.BAT   <ENTER>
CLS
VER

C:\>
```

When you invoke SHOWVER.BAT, DOS clears your screen and displays its version number.

```
C:\> SHOWVER <ENTER>
```

If your batch files are short, you may that find that copying the files from your keyboard is faster than using a word processor to create them.

Creating Batch Files with a Word Processor

Word processors let you create professional quality reports and letters by automatically aligning right and left margins, centering text, and allowing you to use different character fonts. To create such documents, word processors embed in your files special characters that you don't see when you work with the files. Unfortunately, if these special characters are placed in a DOS batch file, DOS cannot understand the characters. Thus, the batch file fails to execute.

Creating Batch Files from Your Keyboard

If your batch files are only a few lines long, you can easily create the file from the keyboard. To accomplish this, use the COPY command with CON as the source.

As an example, assume you want to create a batch file named FILES_A.BAT that displays the files on the disk in drive A. The batch file first clears the screen and then invokes DIR.

To copy the batch file from your keyboard, type the following series of commands and press ENTER at the end of each line:

```
C:\> COPY CON FILES_A.BAT
CLS <ENTER>
DIR A: <ENTER>
```

To tell DOS the batch file is complete, press the F6 function key. DOS displays ^Z (the end-of-file character). When you press ENTER, the FILES_A.BAT file is successfully written.

Most word processors let you create files in document and non-document modes. Some word processors refer to non-document files as ASCII, text, or text-only files. In document mode, the word processor embeds special formatting characters. In ASCII mode, the word processor does not embed the special characters. If you are creating DOS batch files using a word processor, make sure that you create the files in ASCII mode. For more information on creating ASCII files, refer to your word processor's documentation.

Where to Place Your Batch Files

Chapter 6 discussed how DOS directories help you organize your disk by letting you group related files in the same location. Many users create batch files in several different directories and then later have trouble finding the batch file they need. As a solution, create a directory named BATCH.

```
C:\> MKDIR \BATCH
```

Place your commonly used batch files in this directory so you always know where they reside. As discussed in Chapter 9, the PATH command tells DOS the name of directories to search for external commands. By including the BATCH directory within your command path, you can ensure that DOS can locate your batch files, regardless of your current directory. The easiest way to include the BATCH directory within your command path is by using the special batch file called AUTOEXEC.BAT.

Putting AUTOEXEC.BAT to Work for You

One of the most common uses of batch files is to customize the system prompt and define the directories in the command path each time your system starts. To simplify this process, DOS lets you create a special batch file named AUTOEXEC.BAT in your root directory.

AUTOEXEC.BAT is unique from all other batch files because each time your computer starts, DOS automatically locates and executes the commands contained in this special file. AUTOEXEC.BAT must reside in the root directory. You create it in the same manner as other batch files. It contains the names of each command you want DOS to execute when your computer is first started.

If you are using a system installed by someone else, your system may already have an AUTOEXEC.BAT file in the root directory. Use the DIR command to determine if an AUTOEXEC.BAT file exists:

```
C:\> DIR \AUTOEXEC.BAT <ENTER>
```

If the file does exist, use the TYPE command to display the contents of AUTOEXEC.BAT.

```
C:\> TYPE \AUTOEXEC.BAT <ENTER>
```

If the file does not exist, you can create it. If it does exist, do not change the contents of the file until you understand each command in the file.

Common AUTOEXEC.BAT Commands

Two of the most common commands found in AUTOEXEC.BAT are PROMPT (which customizes the system prompt) and PATH (which defines the command path). If your root directory does not contain an AUTOEXEC.BAT file, create the file now and place into it the following commands:

```
PROMPT $P$G
PATH C:\DOS;C:\BATCH
```

If your root directory contains an AUTOEXEC.BAT file, edit the file by using your word processor. Be sure that it has a PROMPT command, and that it includes the directory C:\BATCH in the PATH command.

The tasks accomplished by the PROMPT and PATH commands should not be new to you. PROMPT was discussed in Chapter 6 and PATH was discussed in Chapter 9. If you need a refresher course, refer back to those chapters.

AUTOEXEC.BAT

AUTOEXEC.BAT is a special batch file that enables you to specify one or more commands you want DOS to execute each time your system starts. The AUTOEXEC.BAT file must reside in your root directory.

Using ECHO OFF and @ECHO OFF

By default, when DOS executes a batch file, it displays the name of each command in the batch file as it is executed. For example, if the batch file TIMEDATE.BAT contains the TIME and DATE commands, DOS displays each command name as the command executes.

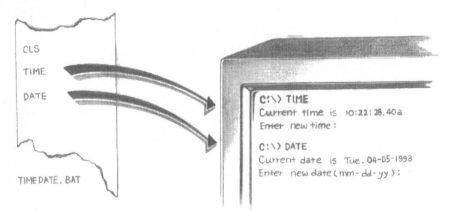

By default, DOS displays the name of each batch file command on your screen as the command executes.

If your batch file contains many commands, the display of each command name may add considerable clutter to your screen. You can place the command ECHO OFF as the first command in your batch files to suppress the display of the names of commands as they are executed. Create the batch file NONAMES.BAT that contains the following commands:

```
ECHO OFF
TIME
DATE
```

When you run NONAMES.BAT, your batch file displays the following:

```
C:\> NONAMES <ENTER>

C:\> ECHO OFF
Current time is 10:22:28.40a
ENTER new time:

Current date is Mon 04-05-1993
ENTER new date (mm-dd-yy):
```

When you include ECHO OFF, DOS does not display each command name. However, DOS does display the message "ECHO OFF" on your screen. If you are using DOS version 3.3 or higher, you can eliminate this message by preceding ECHO OFF with an @ character, as shown here:

```
@ECHO OFF
TIME
DATE
```

In this case, when you invoke the batch file, your screen displays the following:

```
C:\> NONAMES <ENTER>

Current time is 10:22:28.40a
ENTER new time:

Current date is Mon 04-05-1993
ENTER new date (mm-dd-yy):
```

Using @ECHO OFF eliminates the display of command names, as well as the message "ECHO OFF." You will see ECHO OFF or @ECHO OFF in most batch files. Get in the habit of using @ECHO OFF as the first command in your batch files.

Where to Turn Next

DOS batch files have many powerful capabilities not discussed here. In fact, this chapter has only touched on the basics. As you become more experienced with DOS, you can create batch files that can perform decision making—that is, running one set of commands in one situation, and a second set of commands for another. You can also create batch files that repeat a specific DOS command for a specific set of files. To learn how to create such batch files, refer to the book *DOS Inside & Out, Second Edition* or *DOS: The Complete Reference, Fourth Edition*, both from Osborne/McGraw-Hill.

Keys to Success

A batch file is a file you create that contains the name of one or more DOS commands. DOS batch files use the BAT extension. If you type a batch file name at the DOS prompt, DOS locates the batch file on disk and executes (in order) all the commands in the file.

You can create batch files with your word processor, the DOS editor, or by simply copying the batch file from the keyboard. If you are creating batch files with a word processor, make sure you create the batch file in the non-document or ASCII mode.

By default, DOS displays the name of each batch file command as it executes. The ECHO OFF command directs DOS to not display command names. If you are using DOS version 3.3 or higher, precede ECHO OFF with the @ character (@ECHO OFF).

Each time your system starts, DOS searches your root directory for a special batch file named AUTOEXEC.BAT. If this file exists, DOS executes each of the commands contained in the file. AUTOEXEC.BAT allows you to define commands you want to issue each time your system starts.

What Do They Mean by...?

Batch   A batch is a group. In the case of DOS batch files, the group is simply one or more DOS commands.

Command Name Echo   By default, when DOS executes a batch file command, DOS displays the command name on your screen. The process of displaying command names as a batch file executes is called "echoing." The ECHO OFF command disables command name echo.

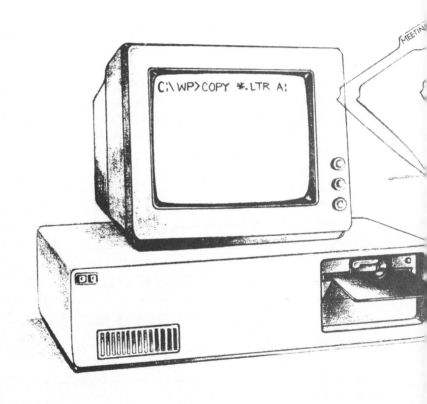

Working with
Groups of Files

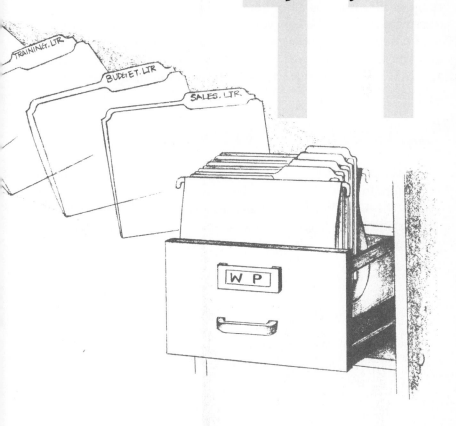

Throughout this book, all of your commands have only worked with one file at a time. For example, in Chapter 8 you used the COPY command to copy one file at a time from your DOS directory to a disk in drive A. When you used the DEL command to delete a file from a directory, you only deleted one file at a time. In many cases, however, you'll want to work with a group of files, such as all of your DOS batch files, or all your word processing documents. To help you perform file operations on a group of files, DOS defines two special *wildcard* characters you can place in your file names when you run a command. When DOS encounters a wildcard character, it replaces the character with the names of all matching files.

The Asterisk (*) Wildcard

Wildcards help you select a group of files. You might want to copy an entire group of files to another disk, or delete a group of files from the current directory. The asterisk wildcard (*) is the most commonly used wildcard. To understand how wildcards work, select the DOS directory and issue the DIR command.

```
C:\> CHDIR \DOS   <ENTER>
C:\DOS> DIR   <ENTER>

Volume in drive C has no label
Volume Serial Number is 1A43-5E8B
Directory of C:\DOS

.               <DIR>      11-23-92   9:26p
..              <DIR>      11-23-92   9:26p
EGA      SYS       4885 01-28-93   6:00a
FORMAT   COM      22717 01-28-93   6:00a
NLSFUNC  EXE       7036 01-28-93   6:00a
COUNTRY  SYS      17066 01-28-93   6:00a
EGA      CPI      58870 01-28-93   6:00a
  :        :         :       :         :
MSCDEX   EXE      25377 01-28-93   6:00a
```

```
RAMDRIVE SYS      5873 01-28-93    6:00a
SMARTDRV EXE     42073 01-28-93    6:00a
COMMAND  COM     52841 01-28-93    6:00a
MOUSE    INI        28 02-03-93   11:54a
        nn file(s)     7527422 bytes
                       9324544 bytes free
```

In this case, DOS displays all the files in the directory. As you can see, DOS displays the names of files with the EXE, COM, and SYS extensions. For example, suppose you want to display a directory listing for only those files with the COM extension. To do so, issue the following DIR command:

```
C:\DOS> DIR *.COM <ENTER>
```

The asterisk wildcard is effectively an "I don't care" symbol. In this case, the asterisk wildcard tells DOS to ignore all of the characters in the file name, matching all the files with the COM extension as shown here:

```
C:\DOS> DIR *.COM  <ENTER>

 Volume in drive C has no label
 Volume Serial Number is 1A43-5E8B
 Directory of C:\DOS

FORMAT   COM     22717 01-28-93    6:00a
KEYB     COM     14983 01-28-93    6:00a
CHOICE   COM      1754 01-28-93    6:00a
EDIT     COM       413 01-28-93    6:00a
  :        :         :     :          :
TREE     COM      6898 01-28-93    6:00a
VSAFE    COM     62576 01-28-93    6:00a
```

```
COMMAND   COM      52841 01-28-93    6:00a
         nn file(s)       321014 bytes
                         9328640 bytes free
```

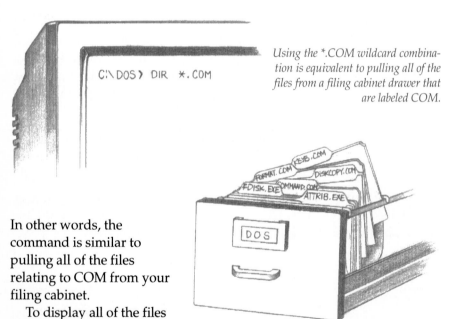

C:\DOS> DIR *.COM

*Using the *.COM wildcard combina-
tion is equivalent to pulling all of the
files from a filing cabinet drawer that
are labeled COM.*

In other words, the
command is similar to
pulling all of the files
relating to COM from your
filing cabinet.

To display all of the files
with the EXE extension,
you would simply change the DIR command to the following:

```
C:\DOS> DIR *.EXE <ENTER>
```

If you use the asterisk wildcard for both the file name and extension, DOS
will match all files in the directory.

```
C:\DOS> DIR *.* <ENTER>
```

In this case, the DIR command corresponds to pulling all of the files from the drawer of the filing cabinet.

All of the DOS file-manipulation commands support wildcards. For example, the following COPY command copies all of the files with the SYS extension to a disk in drive A:

```
C:\DOS> COPY *.SYS A: <ENTER>
```

To fully understand how the asterisk wildcard works, use MKDIR to create the directory TESTDIR, then CHDIR to select TESTDIR as the current directory.

```
C:\DOS> MKDIR \TESTDIR <ENTER>
C:\DOS> CHDIR \TESTDIR <ENTER>
C:\TESTDIR>
```

Next, copy all of the files with the EXE extension from the DOS directory to TESTDIR, as shown here:

```
C:\TESTDIR> COPY \DOS\*.EXE *.EXE <ENTER>
```

Note that both the source and destination file names contain the asterisk wildcard. When the asterisk is used in the destination name, DOS automatically assigns the name of the matching source file to the destination file.

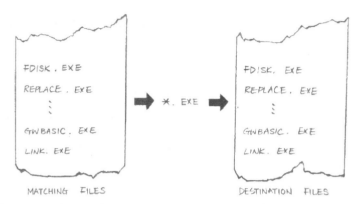

MATCHING FILES   DESTINATION FILES

When you use the asterisk wildcard to specify the destination file name or extension, DOS automatically uses the corresponding name or extension from the source file.

For example, if the file FDISK.EXE resides in the DOS directory, DOS will match FDISK to the *.EXE wildcard and copy the file to the current directory, using the name FDISK.EXE.

Use the DIR command to display the files copied.

```
C:\TESTDIR> DIR   <ENTER>


Volume in drive C has no label
Volume Serial Number is 1A43-5E8B
Directory of C:\TESTDIR

    .            <DIR>      02-15-93   1:29p
    ..           <DIR>      02-15-93   1:29p
NLSFUNC   EXE      7036 01-28-93   6:00a
ATTRIB    EXE     11165 01-28-93   6:00a
CHKDSK    EXE     12908 01-28-93   6:00a
   :        :        :    :         :
MOVE      EXE     17091 01-28-93   6:00a
MSCDEX    EXE     25377 01-28-93   6:00a
SMARTDRV EXE     42073 01-28-93   6:00a
        nn file(s)     3480289 bytes
                       5793792 bytes free
```

Next, again using the COPY command, copy all the files that have the COM extension from the DOS directory to TESTDIR.

```
C:\TESTDIR> COPY \DOS\*.COM *.COM <ENTER>
```

Using the following DIR command, display the names of all files beginning with the letter "D" and having the COM extension:

```
C:\TESTDIR> DIR D*.COM   <ENTER>

 Volume in drive C has no label
 Volume Serial Number is 1A43-5E8B
 Directory of C:\TESTDIR

DOSSHELL COM      4620 01-28-93    6:00a
DISKCOMP COM     10620 01-28-93    6:00a
DISKCOPY COM     11879 01-28-93    6:00a
DOSKEY   COM      5883 01-28-93    6:00a
        4 file(s)       33002 bytes
                      9287680 bytes free
```

In this case, the wildcard tells DOS that in order to match, a file name must begin with the letter "D" and have the extension COM. After the letter "D," you don't care what letters follow.

The wildcard combination of D*.COM tells DOS that in order to match, a file must begin with the letter "D" and have the extension COM.

By changing the DIR command to include the letters "DI" followed by the asterisk wildcard, you reduce the number of matching files to two.

```
C:\TESTDIR> DIR DI*.COM  <ENTER>

Volume in drive C has no label
Volume Serial Number is 1A43-5E8B
Directory of C:\TESTDIR

DISKCOMP COM     10620 01-28-93    6:00a
DISKCOPY COM     11879 01-28-93    6:00a
        2 file(s)        22499 bytes
                       9285632 bytes free
```

Using the DEL command, delete the files in the TESTDIR directory that have the COM extension. Make sure TESTDIR is the current directory before you issue this command.

```
C:\TESTDIR> DEL *.COM <ENTER>
```

A directory listing of TESTDIR reveals that the COM files have been deleted. Next, using the asterisk wildcard for the file name and extension, delete all the files that remain in the TESTDIR directory, as shown here:

```
C:\TESTDIR> DEL *.* <ENTER>
```

In this case, the wildcards tell DOS that you don't care about the file name or the extension. As a result, DOS matches all of the files in the directory. The DEL *.* command can have devastating effects (in other words, deleting all of the files in a directory). Because you might invoke it in error, DEL prompts you to verify that you really want to delete the files:

```
All files in directory will be deleted!
Are you sure (Y/N)?
```

In this case, type **Y** and press ENTER to delete all of the files.

The Asterisk Wildcard (*)

The asterisk wildcard (*) lets you perform DOS file operations on a group of files by specifying "don't care" character positions within the file name or extension. When DOS encounters the asterisk wildcard in a file name, it ignores the character in the position of the asterisk, as well as all of the characters that follow. The following DIR command, for example, displays all the word processing files with the LTR extension that reside in the current directory:

C:\WP51> DIR *.LTR <ENTER>

The Question Mark (?) Wildcard

As you just learned, the DOS asterisk wildcard tells DOS to ignore not only the character in the position containing the wildcard, but also all character positions that follow. In some cases, you may want better control over the files that DOS matches. The question mark wildcard lets you specify a single "don't care" character position.

For example, the following command uses the asterisk wildcard to copy the files that begin with the letter "D" and have the COM extension to the TESTDIR directory.

```
C:\TESTDIR> COPY \DOS\D*.COM *.COM <ENTER>
    4 file(s) copied
```

Under DOS 6, a directory listing reveals that DOS has copied the four files as shown here:

```
C:\TESTDIR> DIR   <ENTER>

 Volume in drive C has no label
 Volume Serial Number is 1A43-5E8B
 Directory of C:\TESTDIR

 .              <DIR>      02-15-93   1:29p
 ..             <DIR>      02-15-93   1:29p
DOSSHELL COM      4620 01-28-93   6:00a
DISKCOMP COM     10620 01-28-93   6:00a
DISKCOPY COM     11879 01-28-93   6:00a
DOSKEY   COM      5883 01-28-93   6:00a
       6 file(s)        33002 bytes
                      9283584 bytes free
```

Assume that you want to delete the two files DISKCOPY.COM and DISKCOMP.COM. You can take advantage of the fact that both files begin with the same six characters. The following DEL command uses two question mark wildcards to tell DOS to delete DISKCOPY.COM and DISKCOMP.COM.

```
C:\TESTDIR> DEL DISKCO??.COM <ENTER>
```

A directory listing reveals that DOS has deleted the two files.

```
C:\TESTDIR> DIR   <ENTER>

 Volume in drive C has no label
 Volume Serial Number is 1A43-5E8B
 Directory of C:\TESTDIR

 .              <DIR>      02-15-93    1:29p
 ..             <DIR>      02-15-93    1:29p
 DOSSHELL COM     4620 01-28-93    6:00a
 DOSKEY   COM     5883 01-28-93    6:00a
         4 file(s)       10503 bytes
                       9304064 bytes free
```

In this case, the question mark wildcards told DOS that, in order to match, a file must begin with the letters DISKCO, and have the extension COM.

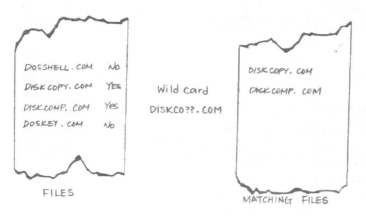

The question mark wildcards tell DOS that a file must begin with DISKCO in order to match.

The Question Mark Wildcard (?)

The question mark wildcard directs DOS to ignore the character in the position containing the wildcard. The following command uses the question mark wildcard to display a directory listing of all files containing a single letter file name:

C:\> DIR ?.* <ENTER>

In this case, the question mark wildcard tells DOS the matching file name can only be one letter long. It does not matter which letter, as long as only one letter is present. The asterisk wildcard in the extension tells DOS you don't care about the matching file name's extension.

Keys to Success

Wildcards let you perform file operations on a group of files. DOS provides two wildcards: the asterisk and the question mark. Both wildcards let you specify "don't care" character positions in the file name and extension.

The asterisk wildcard is the most commonly used wildcard. When DOS encounters the asterisk (in either the file name or extension), it ignores the character in the position containing the wildcard, as well as all characters that follow.

The question mark wildcard directs DOS to ignore a single character position. By combining two or more question mark wildcards, you can attain better control over your file matching.

What Do They Mean by...?

Wildcard Combination   A wildcard combination is any use of either the DOS asterisk (*) or question mark (?) wildcard within a file name. Using wildcard combinations, you can perform DOS commands on a group of files.

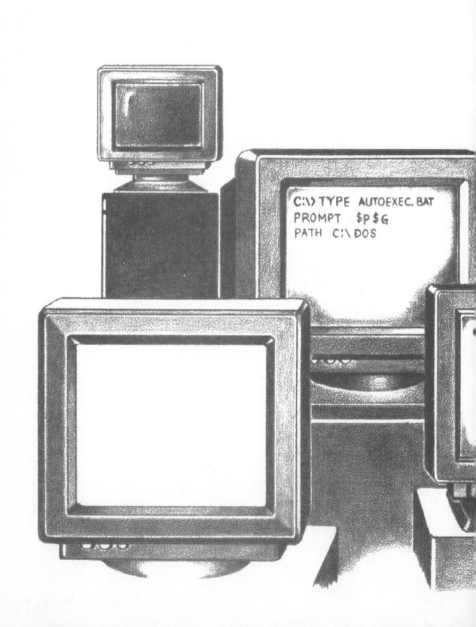

```
C:\> TYPE  AUTOEXEC. BAT
PROMPT  $P $G
PATH  C:\ DOS
```

Customizing
Your System with
CONFIG.SYS

Chapter 10 discussed how DOS searches the root directory for the batch file AUTOEXEC.BAT each time your system starts. If AUTOEXEC.BAT exists, DOS executes the commands listed in the file. Unlike many other DOS files, AUTOEXEC.BAT is unique in that you must create the file yourself.

In addition to AUTOEXEC.BAT, DOS startup procedures use a second user-defined file named CONFIG.SYS. The file's SYS extension indicates the file is a DOS system file. Unlike AUTOEXEC.BAT, which contains one or more commands that DOS executes, CONFIG.SYS contains single-line entries (not commands) that control how DOS works on your system. These single-line entries are sometimes called *directives*. Like AUTOEXEC.BAT, the file CONFIG.SYS must reside in the root directory.

Getting Started with CONFIG.SYS

During the system startup, if DOS locates the file CONFIG.SYS in the root directory, it uses the file's entries to configure itself in memory. If the file does not exist, DOS uses its own default configuration values. If someone else installed DOS on your system for you, that person probably created a CONFIG.SYS file in your root directory. Using the following DIR command, you can determine if the file exists.

```
C:\> DIR CONFIG.SYS <ENTER>
```

If the file exists, you can use the TYPE command to display the contents of the file.

```
C:\> TYPE CONFIG.SYS <ENTER>
```

CONFIG.SYS Versus AUTOEXEC.BAT

Each time your computer starts, DOS searches your disk's root directory for two user-defined files: CONFIG.SYS and AUTOEXEC.BAT. Each serves a distinct purpose. CONFIG.SYS contains one or more entries that define how DOS will configure itself in memory. AUTOEXEC.BAT contains one or more commands that you want DOS to automatically execute each time your system starts.

File	Contents
CONFIG.SYS	System configuration parameters
AUTOEXEC.BAT	DOS commands

If the file does not exist, create the file and place in it the following two entries:

```
FILES=20
BUFFERS=25
```

You can use a word processor to create the CONFIG.SYS file. Or, as you learned in Chapter 10, you can create the file by copying it from your keyboard:

```
C:\> COPY CON CONFIG.SYS <ENTER>
FILES=20 <ENTER>
BUFFERS=25 <ENTER>
^Z <ENTER>
      1 File(s) copied

C:\>
```

The only time DOS uses CONFIG.SYS is during system startup. If you change or add a CONFIG.SYS entry, you must restart DOS for the changes to take effect. In this case, if you create a new CONFIG.SYS file, use the CTRL-ALT-DEL keyboard combination to restart DOS so your changes will take effect.

Assigning the Essential CONFIG.SYS Entries

Although DOS supports several different CONFIG.SYS entries, most users only require two or three essential entries. The FILES= entry tells DOS the number of files a program can open at one time. For most users, the value 20 should be sufficient.

```
FILES=20
```

Many of your application programs (such as a database program or even a word processor) open one or more temporary files behind the scenes. If you don't set the FILES= entry to at least 20, many of these programs will not run properly.

The BUFFERS= entry improves system performance by reducing the number of disk input and output operations DOS must perform to read from or write to a file. Compared to the fast speed of your computer's electronic components, your mechanical disk drives are very slow. By reducing the number of disk operations DOS must perform, you improve the speed of your programs. Most users should find that 25 disk buffers provide excellent performance.

```
BUFFERS=25
```

If another user created your CONFIG.SYS file, it may contain one or more entries which begin with DEVICE=. As a minimum, DOS provides support for the standard hardware found on all computers (such as the screen, keyboard, and printer). If your computer has additional unique hardware (such as a plotter or mouse), the device may require additional software to be present in memory before DOS can access the device. Because this additional software lets DOS control (sometimes called *drive*) the device, the software is called a *device driver*. The DEVICE= entry directs DOS to install a specific device driver into memory. Most CONFIG.SYS files won't require a DEVICE= entry. If your CONFIG.SYS file includes one, now you know why.

Where to Learn More About CONFIG.SYS

As you become more comfortable with DOS, you can learn more about the remaining CONFIG.SYS entries from the books *DOS Inside & Out, Second Edition* and *DOS: The Complete Reference, Fourth Edition*, both available from Osborne/McGraw-Hill. Table 12-1 briefly describes the remaining CONFIG.SYS entries.

Keys to Success

Every time your system starts, DOS searches the root directory for a file named CONFIG.SYS. The CONFIG.SYS file contains one or more single-line entries that DOS uses to customize itself in memory. If CONFIG.SYS does not exist, DOS uses its own default settings.

At a minimum, your CONFIG.SYS file should contain a FILES=20 and a BUFFERS=25 entry. The FILES=20 entry tells DOS that a program can open as many as 20 files at one time. The BUFFERS=25 entry directs DOS to create 25 disk buffers in your computer's fast electronic memory, which in turn reduces the number of slow mechanical disk input and output operations DOS must perform.

Entry	Purpose
BREAK	Enables or disables extended CTRL-BREAK checking
BUFFERS	Specifies the number of disk buffers DOS places in memory
COUNTRY	Defines the country-specific symbol set for international users
DEVICE	Installs a DOS device driver
DEVICEHIGH	Installs a DOS device driver into an upper-memory block
DOS	Installs DOS 5 or 6 into high memory and provides access to upper-memory blocks
DRIVPARM	Defines the characteristics of an external device (typically an external floppy disk)
FCBS	Defines the number of file-control blocks DOS provides to support older applications
FILES	Defines the number of files a program can have open at one time
INSTALL	Directs DOS to load a memory-resident DOS command during system startup (DOS version 4)
LASTDRIVE	Specifies the drive letter of the last logical disk drive DOS supports
MENUCOLOR	Specifies colors for the DOS 6 startup menu
MENUDEFAULT	Specifies the DOS 6 default startup menu option
MENUITEM	Specifies up to 9 entries on the DOS 6 startup menu
NUMLOCK	Controls whether the keyboard's Numlock is initially on or off (DOS 6)
REM	Specifies a comment (or remark)
SHELL	Defines the location and attributes of the command-line interpreter
STACKS	Defines the number of stacks DOS reserves to service hardware interrupts
SWITCHES	Forces an enhanced keyboard to behave as if it is a conventional keyboard
VERIFY	Enables or disables disk verification

Table 12-1. DOS CONFIG.SYS Entries

Many CONFIG.SYS files contain DEVICE= entries that direct DOS to load special software into memory to support a unique hardware device. This special software is called a device driver.

Finally, every time you make a change to CONFIG.SYS, you must restart your system in order for the change to take effect.

What Do They Mean by...?

Device Driver   A software program that lets DOS use a unique hardware device (such as a plotter or mouse). DOS only provides support for the common hardware devices (such as your keyboard, screen, and printer). When you purchase a unique hardware device, the device manufacturer typically provides software that you must install by using the DEVICE= entry in the CONFIG.SYS file.

System Configuration   Before you can use your computer to run other programs, you must run DOS, which then serves as your host while you use your computer. DOS, therefore, always resides in your computer's memory. Depending on your system type and the application programs you run, you may need DOS to support capabilities that other users don't need (for example, you may have a database program that opens 50 files at one time). System configuration is the process of defining different DOS characteristics. The CONFIG.SYS file lets you customize your system configuration. Each time your system starts, DOS uses the contents of CONFIG.SYS to determine the different features it must support. If you don't have a CONFIG.SYS file defined, DOS uses its own default system configuration.

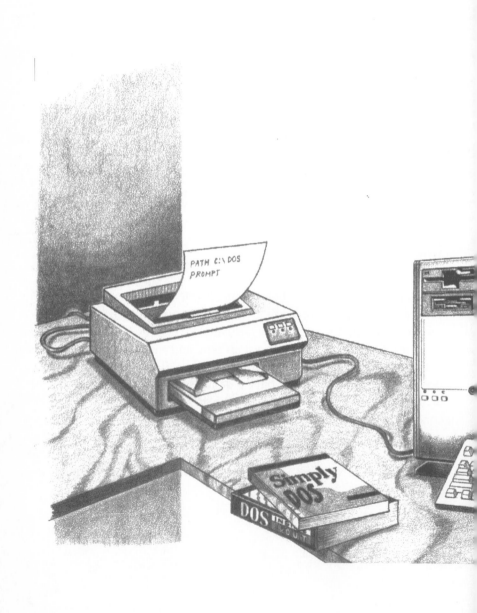

Using DOS to Print

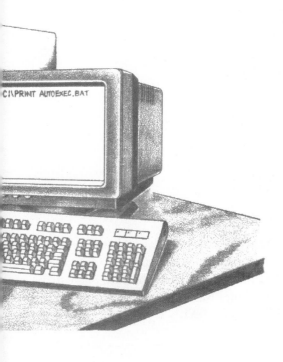

C:\PRINT AUTOEXEC.BAT

If you have a word processing program available, you will probably use it to print the documents that you create. If you don't have a word processor, you can use the PRINT command to print your text files. Recall that Chapter 8 discussed how a text file is a file containing only the standard characters you would expect to see on a page of text. Program files with the extension EXE or COM are not text files. However, the batch files you created in Chapter 10 are text files.

Later in this chapter you will also discover how to print a copy of what appears on your computer screen.

Using the DOS PRINT Command

If you use the DIR command to examine the files in the DOS directory, you will find a file named PRINT.EXE.

```
C:\> DIR \DOS\PRINT.EXE   <ENTER>

 Volume in drive C has no label
 Volume Serial Number is 1A43-5E8B
 Directory of C:\DOS

PRINT     EXE     15640 01-28-93   6:00a
        1 file(s)       15640 bytes
                      9359360 bytes free
```

The PRINT command is an external command that lets you print the contents of one or more files. To send the contents of a file to your printer using PRINT, you simply invoke PRINT and specify the path name to the desired file. For example, the following PRINT command prints the contents of the root directory file AUTOEXEC.BAT:

```
C:\DOS> PRINT \AUTOEXEC.BAT <ENTER>
```

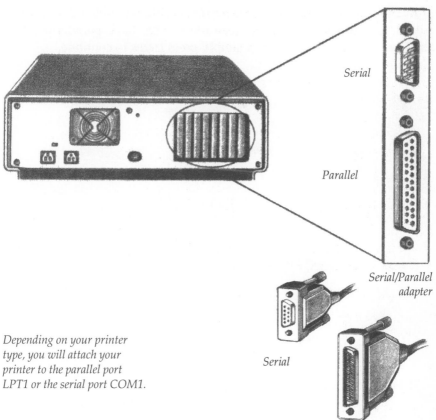

Serial

Parallel

Serial/Parallel
adapter

*Depending on your printer
type, you will attach your
printer to the parallel port
LPT1 or the serial port COM1.*

Serial

Parallel

As discussed in Chapter 1, you
can attach your printer to a serial
or parallel printer port. Because the PRINT
command needs to know which device to use in order to print the file's
contents, PRINT will ask you to type in the device name the first time you
invoke the command.

```
Name of list device [PRN]:
```

Most users attach their printers to the computer's first parallel port. DOS
refers to this parallel port as either LPT1 or PRN. The letters "[PRN]" in the

PRINT prompt tell you that if you press ENTER, PRINT will send the printer output to the device PRN. Because most users have parallel printers attached to this port, most users simply press ENTER to continue.

```
C:\> PRINT FILENAME. EXT
Name of list device [PRN] : <ENTER>
```

```
C:\> PRINT FILENAME. EXT
Name of list device [PRN] : COM1 <ENTER>
```

If your printer is attached to the parallel port LPT1, you can press ENTER at the PRINT prompt for a list device. If your printer is attached to a serial port (such as COM1), you must type in the device name.

If you have a serial printer attached to a serial communications port such as COM1 or COM2, you must type in the serial port name before pressing ENTER.

If you aren't sure which printer port you are using, the port is probably PRN. To verify the printer port, examine the type of cable connected to your printer.

When you press ENTER, PRINT should display a message telling you that it is printing the file. If your printer does not begin printing, first make sure the printer is turned on and the printer's on-line light is illuminated. Second, make sure PRINT found the file you want to print and did not display the message **File not found**. If your printer is attached to a serial port such as COM1, you may need to issue a MODE command that tells DOS the printer's correct speed. For more information on the correct MODE command, refer to your printer documentation.

The PRINT Command

The PRINT command lets you print the contents of one or more text files. To use PRINT, specify the complete path name to the file in the PRINT command line. For example, the following command prints the contents of the root directory file CONFIG.SYS.

C:\DOS> PRINT \CONFIG.SYS <ENTER>

The first time you use it, PRINT prompts you to enter the device name to which your printer is attached. Most users can use the default device name PRN by simply pressing ENTER. Users whose printers are attached to a serial port (such as COM1) must enter the correct serial port name.

Printing More Than One File

Although your printer is only capable of printing one file at a time, the PRINT command lets you tell DOS the names of several files that you want to print, one immediately after another. When you include two or more file names in the PRINT command line, PRINT sends each file's contents to the printer in the same order in which you specify the file names. For example, the following PRINT command instructs DOS to print the file AUTOEXEC.BAT followed by the file CONFIG.SYS.

```
C:\DOS> PRINT \AUTOEXEC.BAT \CONFIG.SYS <ENTER>
```

Because your printer can only print one file's contents at a time, PRINT begins printing the first specified file, while placing the name of each additional file in a list called the *print queue*. Using the previous command as an example, DOS begins printing the file AUTOEXEC.BAT and places the file CONFIG.SYS in the queue. PRINT displays a message telling the status of each file, as shown here:

```
C:\DOS> PRINT \AUTOEXEC.BAT \CONFIG.SYS <ENTER>

  C:\AUTOEXEC.BAT is currently being printed
  C:\CONFIG.SYS is in queue

C:\>
```

When the file AUTOEXEC.BAT has been printed, PRINT ejects that page from your printer and begins printing the file CONFIG.SYS at the top of a new page.

Working While Your Files Print

The PRINT command is unique from other DOS commands in that, while your files print, you can continue to execute other commands from the DOS prompt. Thus, if you have to print a long file, you are still free to use your computer to perform other tasks. In so doing, PRINT helps you get the most from your computer.

The DOS PRINT command lets you run other DOS commands at the same time that your files print.

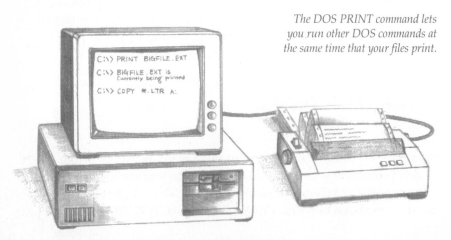

Printing Your Screen's Current Contents

The PRINT command lets you print the contents of an existing text file. In some cases, however, you may want to print the current contents of your screen. For example, assume you are running an application program and don't understand the current screen or an error message appearing on the screen. By printing the screen's current contents, you can refer back to the message to discuss the problem with another user.

To print the current screen contents, hold down the SHIFT key and press the PRTSC key. When you do so, your printer should begin printing the screen's contents. Because printing the screen's contents doesn't require a complete printed page, you may have to press your printer's Form Feed button to eject the page from your printer.

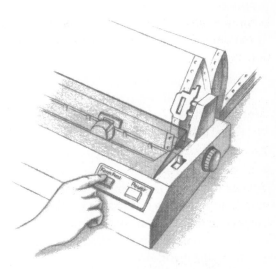

To eject a page from your printer, press the Form Feed button.

Keys to Success

The PRINT command is an external command that lets you print the contents of one or more text files. To print a file using PRINT, you must specify a complete path name to the file or files you want to print.

If you specify multiple files for printing, PRINT will begin printing the first file specified and will place the names of the remaining files into a list called a print queue. As one file finishes printing, PRINT selects the next file in the print queue for printing.

In some cases, you may want to print the current contents of your screen display. The SHIFT-PRTSC keyboard combination directs DOS to print the current screen contents.

What Do They Mean by...?

List Device   A list device is another name for your printer port. Most DOS users connect their parallel printers to the port LPT1. DOS lets you refer to this device name as LPT1 or PRN. If your printer is attached to a serial port, your list device is probably COM1 or COM2.

Queue   A queue is a list. When you use the PRINT command to print a file, PRINT will begin printing one file while placing the names of the remaining files in a list, or print queue. When it finishes printing one file's contents, PRINT removes the next file name from the queue and begins printing its contents.

Screen Dump   A screen dump is a printed copy of the screen's current contents. Using the SHIFT-PRTSC keyboard combination, you can print your screen contents. When you experience errors while running an application program, many manufacturers will ask you to create a screen dump showing the error.

Making Backup
Copies of Your
Files

One of the worst experiences new users encounter is losing an important file because of an errant DOS command, or worse yet, losing all their files because the disk fails. To reduce the chance of such data loss, you must make backup copies of your files and then store the copies in a safe location. This chapter presents the steps you must regularly perform to back up your files.

Understanding Disk Backups

In general, there are two backup operations you must perform. Once a month, ideally on the first day of the month, you should back up every file on your disk. Because this complete disk backup can be time-consuming, you need to do it just once a month.

Perform a complete disk backup once a month to back up every file on your disk.

At the end of each day, you should perform a much faster backup of only those files you created or changed that day.

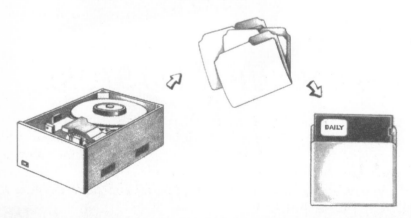

At the end of each day, you must back up only those files you created or changed that day.

Should you later delete or overwrite files you need, or should your disk fail, you can perform a file-restore operation to place the backed-up files onto a hard disk.

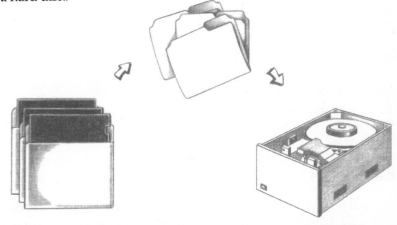

A file-restore operation copies one or more files from a backup floppy onto a hard disk.

For the past 10 years, users have used the DOS BACKUP and RESTORE commands to perform disk and file backup and restore operations. DOS 6, however, introduced the MSBACKUP command, a very powerful backup program. This chapter presents both methods.

Before you get started, you will want to purchase a disk storage container to hold only your backup disks.

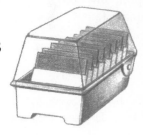

Store your backup disks in a disk container that you place in a safe location.

Using BACKUP and RESTORE

If you are not using DOS 6, you must use the DOS BACKUP and RESTORE commands. Both BACKUP and RESTORE are very powerful, and they support many different options. This chapter presents only the information you'll need to get your backup job done.

Before you begin, issue the following MKDIR command to create a subdirectory named BACKUP.

```
C:\> MKDIR C:\BACKUP   <ENTER>
```

The BACKUP commands you will issue to back up
your disks will create a log file that specifies which
files reside on each backup disk. The log file will have
the name BACKUP.LOG and will reside in the
BACKUP directory. If you ever need to restore a
specific file, you can quickly determine which backup
disk contains the file, by using the log file.

Backing Up Your Entire Disk

Once a month, you should back up all the files on your hard disk. Because your
hard disk is quite large, the disk backup may require considerable time and
quite a few floppies. However, backing up your entire disk will be well worth
your time and effort should you ever need your backup files. To calculate how
many floppy disks you will need, invoke the CHKDSK command:

```
C:\> CHKDSK   <ENTER>

Volume MSDOS 5      created 09-17-1992 7:37p
Volume Serial Number is 1931-9E01

104515584 bytes total disk space
    73728 bytes in 2 hidden files
    43008 bytes in 17 directories
 18395136 bytes in 564 user files
 86003712 bytes available on disk

     2048 bytes in each allocation unit
    51033 total allocation units on disk
    41994 available allocation units on disk

   655360 total bytes memory
   592480 bytes free
```

To determine the amount of disk space in use, subtract the number of available bytes from the total disk space:

Bytes in use = Total disk space – Available space

Using the previous CHKDSK command, the equation becomes the following:

Bytes in use =104,515,584 – 86,003,712
=18,511,872

Next, to determine the number of floppies required, divide the bytes in use by the size of your floppy disk, as listed in Table 14-1:

$$\text{Number of floppies} = \frac{\text{Bytes in use}}{\text{Floppy storage capacity}}$$

Disk Size	Storage Capacity
360KB	362,496 bytes
720KB	730,112 bytes
1.2MB	1,213,952 bytes
1.44MB	1,457,664 bytes
2.88MB	2,915,328 bytes

Table 14-1.   *Disk Storage Capacities*

If you are using 1.44MB floppies, the disk previously displayed by CHKDSK will require 13 floppy disks:

$$\text{Number of floppies} = \frac{18,511,872}{1,457,664}$$

$$= 12.7$$
$$= 13$$

Using the steps presented in Chapter 7, format the number of floppies necessary for backing up all the information currently residing on your hard disk. Do not include the /S (system disk) switch in the Format command:

```
C:\> FORMAT A: <ENTER>
```

After you have the proper number of floppies, issue the following BACKUP command to back up every file on your hard disk:

```
C:\> BACKUP  C:\*.* A: /S /L:C:\BACKUP\BACKUP.LOG  <ENTER>
```

BACKUP will display the following message, prompting you to place an unused disk into drive A:

```
Insert backup diskette 01 in drive A:

WARNING! Files in the target drive
A:\ root directory will be erased
Press any key to continue . . .
```

Place one of your newly formatted floppies in drive A and press ENTER. BACKUP begins copying files to drive A, displaying each file name on your screen. Eventually the floppy disk in drive A becomes full, and BACKUP prompts you to insert a new disk in drive A. Continue this process until your backup operation is complete. Finally, assign a label to each backup disk; the label should indicate the backup date and the disk's number.

Label each backup floppy with the backup date and the floppy's number.

At the start of the next month, perform these same steps to back up your hard disk. If the backup successfully completes, replace the previous month's complete disk and daily backup floppies with the new set. You can now reuse the previous month's backup floppies.

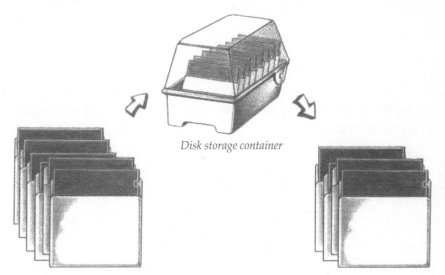

Disk storage container

After finishing a complete disk backup, replace the previous month's floppies with your current disks.

Backing Up Changed or Newly Created Files

If users always had to perform complete disk backups, they would stop doing backups just because of the time involved. Luckily, after you perform a complete disk backup, for the next 30 days you only have to back up those files whose contents you have changed, along with any new files. These daily backups are very easy and quick. The day after you perform your complete disk backup, place a formatted floppy disk in drive A and issue the following BACKUP command:

```
C:\> BACKUP C:\*.* A: /S /A /M /L:C\BACKUP.LOG  <ENTER>
```

BACKUP prompts you to place a floppy disk in drive A:

```
Insert last backup diskette in drive A:
Press any key to continue . . .
```

Place a formatted disk in drive A and press ENTER. Depending on the number and size of files you have created or changed, the backup may require more than one disk. Label your daily backup with the date and the disk's number.

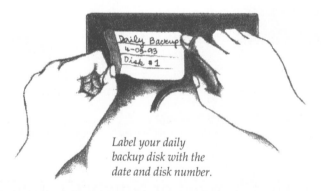

Label your daily backup disk with the date and disk number.

On the days that follow, issue the BACKUP command just shown. When BACKUP prompts you for a disk, insert the last disk you used for the previous day's backup. If there is space on the disk, BACKUP will use it. If the disk is full, BACKUP will prompt you to insert a new disk.

Restoring One or More Files

Backup disks are like insurance. Hopefully you will never need to use them. But if you should need one or more files stored on your backup disks, use the RESTORE command. The following sections discuss the steps you must follow to restore a specific file, directory, or even your entire disk.

Restoring a Specific File   To restore one or more specific files, first print a copy of the backup log file:

```
C:\> PRINT C:\BACKUP\BACKUP.LOG  <ENTER>
```

Next, search the log file for the last reference of the desired file name. Note the number of the disk containing the file.

Place the corresponding disk in drive A and issue the following RE-STORE command, replacing DIRNAME and FILENAME.EXT with your file's name and directory:

```
C:\> RESTORE A: C:\DIRNAME\FILENAME.EXT  <ENTER>
```

RESTORE prompts you to insert backup disk number one:

```
Insert backup diskette 01 in drive A:
Press any key to continue . . .
```

Place the backup disk containing the file you desire in drive A and press ENTER. If the disk containing the file is not disk number one, RESTORE displays a message stating such. Press ENTER to continue. RESTORE copies the file to your disk. If the file is very large, RESTORE may prompt you to insert an additional backup floppy disk.

Restoring an Entire Directory   To restore an entire directory as well as its subdirectories, issue the following RESTORE command, substituting DIRNAME with the desired directory name:

```
C:\> RESTORE A: C:\DIRNAME\*.* /S  <ENTER>
```

RESTORE displays the prompt shown here, instructing you to place the first backup disk in drive A. Place disk number one of your monthly backup disks in drive A and press ENTER. RESTORE prompts you to insert various disks. Follow RESTORE's prompts for each of your monthly backup disks. When RESTORE ends, repeat the previous RESTORE command, inserting each of your daily backup disks.

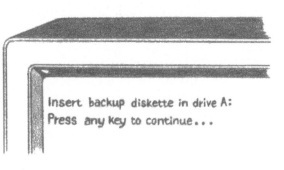

Insert backup diskette in drive A:
Press any key to continue...

Restoring an Entire Disk   If you have to restore an entire hard disk, you will probably need a floppy disk containing the RESTORE command. Place the disk in drive A and issue the following RESTORE command:

```
A> RESTORE A: C:\*.* /S  <ENTER>
```

RESTORE prompts you for the first backup disk. Place the first monthly backup disk in drive A and press ENTER. RESTORE prompts you to insert each monthly backup disk. When RESTORE ends, repeat this process for your daily backup disks.

Using the DOS 6 MSBACKUP Command

DOS 6 provides the powerful MSBACKUP backup utility, whose capabilities far exceed what can be discussed in this book. As before, this section discusses the steps you must follow to perform essential backup and restore operations.

Performing Disk Backup Operations

The DOS 6 MSBACKUP command is a menu-driven backup utility. Invoke MSBACKUP from the DOS prompt:

```
C:\> MSBACKUP  <ENTER>
```

MSBACKUP displays its main menu:

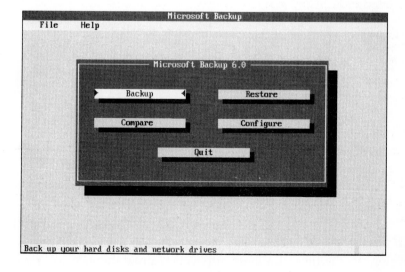

Using your keyboard arrow keys, highlight the BACKUP option and press ENTER. MSBACKUP displays its Backup screen:

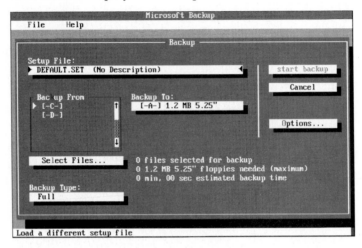

MSBACKUP lets you create setup files that define which files to back up, as well as the backup type (complete disk or daily). In this case, you will create two setup files, one for a monthly backup and one for daily backup.

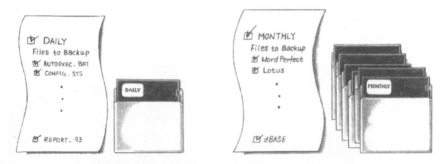

A daily setup file will control your daily backup, and the monthly file will backup your entire disk.

One of MSBACKUP's nicest features is that it allows you to select the specific files you want to back up. You don't have to invest time and disks backing up the files of a large application program such as Windows, which you can reinstall if necessary.

Creating a Monthly Backup Setup File   To create a monthly backup, press TAB to select the disk you want to back up (probably drive C) and the disk to which MSBACKUP will copy the backup files (probably drive A). Next, use TAB to highlight the Select Files option and press ENTER. MSBACKUP displays a copy of your directory tree:

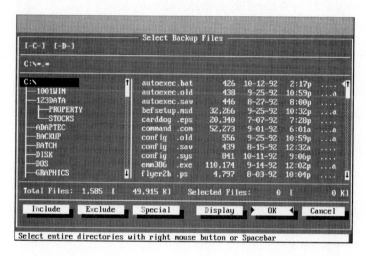

To select the files in a specific directory for backing up, use your keyboard arrow keys to highlight the directory name, and press SPACEBAR. MSBACKUP places checkmarks before each file's name appearing in the directory list, to indicate that it will back up the file. Perform these steps to select the files in each directory you want to back up. After your have selected the files, press TAB to highlight the OK option and press ENTER. MSBACKUP redisplays its Backup menu. Press TAB to highlight the Backup Type option and press ENTER. MSBACKUP displays the Backup Type menu shown here:

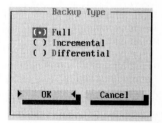

Use your arrow keys to highlight the Full option and press SPACEBAR. Press TAB to highlight OK and press ENTER. MSBACKUP returns you to the Backup menu.

Press the ALT-F keyboard combination.
MSBACKUP displays the File menu:

Use your arrow keys to highlight the Save Setup
As option, and then press ENTER. MSBACKUP
displays the Save Setup File menu, as shown here:

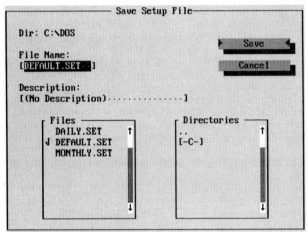

Type the file name **MONTHLY.SET** and press ENTER. MSBACKUP
redisplays its Backup menu. Your monthly setup file is ready for use.

Creating a Daily Backup Setup File   The process of creating a daily
setup file is almost identical to the steps you just performed. When
MSBACKUP displays the Backup Type menu, however, select Incremental. Likewise, when MSBACKUP displays the Save Setup File menu, type
the file name **DAILY.SET**.

Performing a Monthly Backup Operation   To perform a monthly
backup operation, start MSBACKUP and select the Backup option. When
MSBACKUP displays its Backup menu, highlight the Setup File option and
press ENTER. MSBACKUP displays the Setup File menu, as follows:

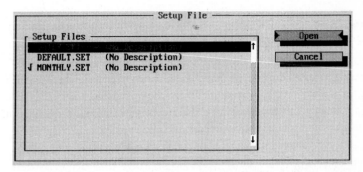

Use your arrow keys to highlight the file name MONTHLY.SET, and then press SPACEBAR followed by ENTER. MSBACKUP displays its Backup menu. In the lower-right corner of your screen, MSBACKUP displays information describing the number of files to be backed up, the number of floppies required, and the anticipated time required. Press TAB to highlight the Start Backup option and press ENTER. MSBACKUP prompts you to insert a disk into the disk drive. Do so and press ENTER. MSBACKUP begins copying files to the disk, displaying status information on your screen describing the operation. Eventually the floppy disk fills and MSBACKUP prompts you to insert another. As you remove a backup disk, attach a label to the disk that contains the date and the disk's number.

After the backup completes, MSBACKUP displays the Backup Complete message box, shown here:

Attach labels to your disks that show the date and disk number.

```
┌─────── Backup Complete ───────┐
│                               │
│  Selected  files:      155    │
│  Backed up files:      155    │
│  Skipped:                0    │
│                               │
│  Disks:                  1    │
│  Bytes:            619,986    │
│                               │
│  Total Time:          0:27    │
│  Your Time:           0:12    │
│  Backup Time:         0:15    │
│                               │
│  KBytes Per Min:     2,476    │
│  Compression:          1.7    │
│                               │
│       ▶   OK   ◀              │
│                               │
└───────────────────────────────┘
```

Press ENTER. MSBACKUP displays its main menu. Select Quit to return to DOS.

Performing a Daily Backup Operation

To perform a daily backup operation, start MSBACKUP and select the Backup option.

When MSBACKUP displays its Backup menu, highlight the Setup File option and press ENTER. When MSBACKUP displays the Setup File menu, use your arrow keys to highlight the file name DAILY.SET and press SPACEBAR followed by ENTER. MSBACKUP displays its Backup menu. As before, the lower-right corner of your screen displays specifics about the number of files it will back up, the number of disks required, and the anticipated amount of time the backup will require.

Press TAB to highlight the Start Backup option and press ENTER. MSBACKUP prompts you to insert a disk into a disk drive. By default, the DOS BACKUP command places each day's backups on separate disks. As such, place a formatted disk in the disk drive and press ENTER. MSBACKUP displays status information describing the backup. Depending on the size and number of files, MSBACKUP may prompt you to insert additional disks.

As you remove one disk, attach a label that contains the backup date and disk number.

When the backup completes, MSBACKUP displays an informational message describing the backup. Press ENTER. MSBACKUP displays its main menu. Select Quit.

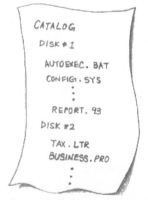

Attach a label to each disk describing the backup date and disk number.

Restoring Files

Each time you perform a backup operation, MSBACKUP creates a catalog describing each of the files backed up. By default, MSBACKUP stores the catalog files in the DOS directory.

MSBACKUP catalog files track which files have been backed up.

If you perform backups on a daily basis, you will quickly develop many catalog files. MSBACKUP refers to this collection of catalog files as a catalog set.

When you need to restore one or more files, search through the catalog set until you find the most recent backup of the files. The catalog file name indicates from which disk you will restore the files.

When you perform a complete disk backup, MSBACKUP removes the previous catalog files, allowing you to easily start the next month's backups. The following sections describe the steps to follow to restore specific files, a directory, or your entire disk.

Restoring Specific Files or a Directory   To restore specific files, start MSBACKUP from the DOS prompt and select Restore. MSBACKUP displays the Restore menu:

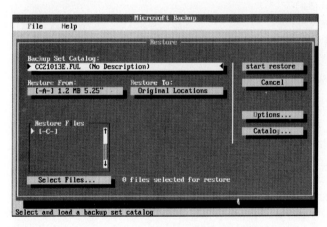

Press TAB to highlight Backup Set Catalog and press ENTER. MSBACKUP displays the list of catalog files, as shown in the following:

Highlight the file named DAILY.CAT and press the SPACEBAR followed
by ENTER. Press TAB to select files and press ENTER. MSBACKUP displays
the directory entries and files available on the backup disks:

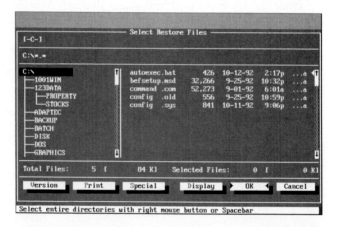

Use your arrow keys to highlight files or directories and press the SPACEBAR
to select them for restoration. Press TAB to select OK. Press ENTER.
MSBACKUP displays the Restore menu. Press TAB to highlight Start Restore. Press ENTER. MSBACKUP prompts you to place specific backup disks
in drive A. Do so and press ENTER. When the operation completes,
MSBACKUP displays a status message. Press ENTER. MSBACKUP returns
you to its main menu.

   If MSBACKUP did not list the files you need to restore, repeat the
previous process, using the file MONTHLY.CAT instead of DAILY.CAT.

Restoring Your Entire Disk   To restore your entire disk, start MS-BACKUP and select Restore. If the catalog files exist, follow the steps discussed in the previous section to first restore all the files listed in MONTHLY.CAT. If the catalog files do not exist, you must first build them, which is a process whose difficulty falls outside of the scope of this book. For a detailed description of this process, refer to the Osborne/McGraw-Hill book, *DOS: The Complete Reference, Fourth Edition.*

What Do They Mean by...?

Complete Disk Backup   A backup operation that backs up every file on your disk.

Daily Backup   A backup operation that backs up only those files you have created or changed since the last backup. Also called an incremental backup.

E